CARDINAL IDEAS OF JEREMIAH

CARDINAL IDEAS OF JEREMIAH

BY

CHARLES E. JEFFERSON

New York

THE MACMILLAN COMPANY

1928

PRINTED IN THE UNITED STATES OF AMERICA
BY THE STRATFORD PRESS, INC.

PREFACE

This is a companion volume of my book *Cardinal Ideas of Isaiah* published some three years ago. The cordial reception given to the former volume encourages me to offer this one to the public.

I cannot help feeling that the Hebrew prophets are largely neglected both by the ministers and the laymen of our churches. To the average layman, the prophets are a sealed book. The reason is that the preacher does not break the seal. The prophets, it must be admitted, are not easy reading, and without an interpreter, their message is largely unintelligible. To understand them one must possess the historic background. Only a student who has time and patience to dig out of commentaries and dictionaries and encyclopedias the needed information, is able to present their ideas in a form which will prove serviceable to our generation. When once understood, the prophets turn out to be thoroughly modern men. They were obliged to deal with the same sort of social and religious problems with which Christian men are to-day grappling. They are wonderfully up to date when one breaks through the crust of their antique language.

PREFACE

To the preacher they are full of suggestion and inspiration, and to the layman they furnish instruction and guidance which can be found nowhere else. They supplement the New Testament most admirably at the very point at which it is most in need of being supplemented.

I would not say that Jeremiah is the greatest of the prophets of Israel, but I have no hesitation in asserting that he is one of the three greatest. The First Isaiah, Jeremiah, and the Second Isaiah are the three men of the Old Testament whom every Christian ought to know. The Christian Church is to-day in lamentable need of the special help which the Hebrew prophets are able to give.

The sermons of this volume were preached in the Broadway Tabernacle in the winter and spring of 1928, and are now given to a larger circle with the hope that many a minister and not a few Bible School Teachers may be stimulated by them to a larger use of the prophets in the discussion of the tangled and vexing problems of our day.

C. E. J.

Broadway Tabernacle,
New York, July, 1928.

CONTENTS

CARDINAL IDEAS OF JEREMIAH

Cardinal Ideas of Jeremiah

I

THE MAN JEREMIAH

Most of us do not think of Jeremiah as a man. The name suggests a book. We know there is a book by the name of Jeremiah, and that it is somewhere in the Old Testament. Some of us have not read it for years, but we are sure it is in the Bible, and it gives us satisfaction to know that it is there. We do not read the book but we believe it is inspired and we would not allow anybody to remove the book from the Bible. If any school of theology in this country should decide to cut out the Book of Jeremiah, or if any company of scholars in England should decide that Jeremiah is unworthy of a place in the Old Testament Canon, we should rise in indignation and feel that an outrage had been perpetrated on us all. We do not read the book but we want it in the Bible. We do not read it but we want it in the house. We do not care whether it is in our mind or not but we want it in the house. We are just superstitious enough to believe that it helps us to have it in the house whether we have it in our mind or not.

Probably we should read the book more if we knew more about the man. There would have been no book if there had been no man. Every book comes out of a man. As John Milton said long ago, "A good book is the lifeblood of a master spirit." Behind the book Jeremiah there stands the man Jeremiah, and it is about the man we are to think awhile to-day.

We talk sometimes about the prophet Jeremiah and call him one of the major prophets, but even then we are not thinking of the man. We call certain prophets "major" prophets because we are thinking of certain books. The major prophets are bigger books. The minor prophets are smaller books. By major prophet we do not mean that the man is a bigger man physically or mentally or spiritually than a so-called minor prophet. All we mean is that he is the author of a bigger book.

Even when we use the word "prophet" we do not ordinarily think of a man like ourselves. A prophet was a man to whom God said things, and God does not say anything to anybody nowadays, and so a prophet was not like anybody whom

we know. He was not at all like us. He belonged
in a class all by himself. He was a sort of human poll-parrot. God said something and the
parrot repeated what God said. Many persons
have that idea of a prophet. A prophet was
a phonograph. God spoke into it and the phonograph spoke out what God had spoken in. That
is the popular idea of a prophet. A prophet was
a harp, and God smote the strings of the harp
and they gave forth a certain kind of music. It
may be some of us have had that idea of a
prophet. So long as that is our idea we can never
come close to a prophet. Between us and him
there is a great gulf fixed, and we cannot pass over
to him nor can he pass over to us.

The aim of my sermon is to help you realize
that Jeremiah was a man, and a man very much
like ourselves. I want to make the Book of Jeremiah live. I can conceive of no greater work for
a preacher than the work of making the Bible
live. We read magazines because they are alive.
We read biographies and novels because they are
throbbing with life. Many persons do not read
the Bible, and the reason is that the Bible is dead.
You cannot induce people to read a dead book.
If people are to read the Bible somebody must
make it live. That is the great business of the
preacher. The men of the Bible do not help

us and cannot help us if these men are dead. Only live men can bring us help. To many of us Jeremiah is a dead man. He has never helped us in our difficulties or comforted us in our sorrows or inspired us in our dejection. He is one of the greatest men who ever lived, one of the most wonderful of all the Hebrew prophets, and yet he has never helped us. The world is no different to us because he lived, and our life has not been changed by anything he said or did. What a tragedy that such a man should stand within our reach, able and willing to help us, while we go on living as though he had never been born. He does not help us because he is dead. My purpose is to raise him from the dead. I want to bring him out of the tomb. I am going to cause him to stand up before you so that you can feel his heart beat and hear him breathe. I want you to know him so that he can become your companion, and you and he can walk together along life's difficult and checkered way.

I imagine the feeling of protest which must run through your hearts at the mention of my subject—Jeremiah. I can almost hear some of you saying, "Why does he want to take a boresome subject like that? Why does he not deal with some man now alive or who has been dead only a little time? Why go back thousands of

years and dig up that old antediluvian when there
are so many interesting and inspiring men now
alive? And why go back to a world which has
vanished? Why turn one's back on a world which
is bristling with fascinating questions and baffling
problems and waste one's time on a world which
is dead? All the nations with which Jeremiah
had to do are dead. Nineveh is dead, and so is
Babylon, and so is Memphis, and so is Thebes,
and so are Tyre and Sidon, and so are Elam and
Edom and Kedar and Hazor and Media and
Moab and Lydia and all the rest. All the nations which Jeremiah knew have dissolved, and
'like an insubstantial pageant faded have left not
a rack behind.' Why go back to a world which
has vanished and which can never come again?
All these dead nations are in their sarcophaguses.
Why disturb their ashes?"

The question is plausible, and this is my answer:
It is not true that that ancient world has passed
away. Its external features have changed but the
heart of that world lives in the present. God
has not changed in the last twenty-five hundred
years. He is the same yesterday, to-day and
forever. Man has not changed in his essential
nature and character within the last twenty-five
hundred years. The relation of man to God and
the relation of man to man have not changed

since the days of Jeremiah, and therefore the fundamental problems of the world are the same to-day that they have always been. The perplexities by which we are puzzled are the perplexities by which men were bewildered in the sixth century before Christ. All the vices and crimes are old. They have not changed in twenty-five hundred years. Make a list of the crimes and vices reported in our newspapers and you can match it with a similar list to be found in the Book of Jeremiah. The vices and crimes are all ancient and so are the virtues and graces. They all blossomed in the morning of the world. And so I am not going to conduct you into a world that has vanished, or ask you to think of a man who is dead. His body has been dead for twenty-five hundred years but we can see him all the better because he stands so far from us. We cannot see distinctly men who are alive. There is a mist over their faces. We see them through our prejudices and misunderstandings and passions. We cannot see Stresemann or Briand or Chamberlain or Borah as distinctly as men will see them fifty years from now. We can see Lincoln more clearly than we can see Roosevelt or Wilson because Lincoln has been dead for sixty-two years; and we can see Washington more clearly than Lincoln because Washington has been dead twice

[6]

as long. It is a great advantage to look at a man twenty-five hundred years away from our time. The controversies have ceased, the fires of passion have died down, the prejudices have lost their magic power to pervert and distort. We can see the man as he was and can receive the message which he has to deliver.

Let me remind you that he was a man of like passion as ourselves. He was tempted in all points even as we are, and like us he also sinned. At the beginning of his public career he had a tremendous conflict. He was a young man in his early twenties. His eyes were keen. There are no keener eyes on the earth than are the eyes of young men in the early twenties. He saw that the world was not right. He realized that society was corrupt. He knew that his country was on the down grade. He was sure that some one should stand up and speak for the truth and the right. He felt he ought to do this, but he shrank from doing it. There was a dialogue in his soul. He had two voices within him, the higher voice and the lower voice. The higher voice always says, "You ought to stand up for the truth. You ought to defend the right. You ought to be on God's side. You ought to make this beautiful and difficult piece of work your own." But the other voice says, "You need not do it. Let some-

[7]

body else do it. Some one else can do it better than you."

That was the experience which came to Moses. There were two conflicting voices within him. He felt his people ought to be delivered from bondage. Some one ought to protect them against the tyranny of Pharaoh. Some one ought to meet that despot face to face. But there was a voice in the heart of Moses which kept saying, "You are not the man to do this work. You are not fitted for it. You are no talker. You have a clumsy tongue. It takes an eloquent man to carry out successfully an enterprise like this." The lower voice was persuasive and persistent, but it did not prevail. Isaiah had a similar experience. When he was in the early twenties he was deeply stirred by the condition of his country. The tone of society was low. The fabric of social life was corrupt. The political condition of the capital was rotten. He knew that something must be done. Some brave voice must speak out. Some heroic patriot must stand up for the right. God is a holy God, and therefore some one must plead for holy living. A voice within him said, "You are the man to do it! Why don't you do it? You ought to do it!" But another voice in his heart said, "You are not fit to do it. You are not good enough. What impertinence for a man

[8]

to condemn sin in his fellow man when he has so much sin in his own heart! A man as sinful as you are ought to keep silence. Let a saint plead for holiness in the hearts of the people." Thus spoke the lower voice, but it did not prevail.

A like experience came to Jeremiah. He felt that his nation had reached a crisis, that some one must cry out against the social evils of his city. He felt that he ought to do it. No one else was willing to do it, and so the responsibility was rolled on him. But a voice within him said, "You are not old enough. You lack the age and wisdom. The social problem is a complex one, and only men of long experience can grapple with it." The lower voice was persuasive and persistent, but it did not prevail. The prophet felt he was called to speak for God and speak he did.

The two voices speak in every human heart. One voice always says: "You ought to stand up for the right. You ought to speak for the truth. You ought to be loyal to the highest. You ought to be faithful to God. You ought to take up that difficult piece of work and do it for the sake of the town." A second voice answers: "You ought not to do it. You are not fitted for it. You are not a speaker. You are not good enough. You are not old enough." Through the first half of

[9]

life the voice says, "You are not old enough." Through the last half of life the voice says, "You are too old." Sometimes the voice says, "You are not well enough educated. You don't know enough." Often it says, "You are too busy. Let somebody do it who has more time." And so all over the country in all of our churches there are men and women who have listened to the lower voice, and to-day are not doing anything which is difficult and fine.

The prophet having conquered one temptation had to face others. After he had followed his work for a season, he was tempted to give it up. It was too hard. It was harder than he had expected. He was in deep water, far deeper than he had anticipated. He had no idea he would have to pay so big a price. It never occurred to him the burden would be so heavy or the road would be so rough. And so he decided to give up his work. He made a vow one day that never again would he speak for God. But he did not keep his vow. He told Baruch one day: "If I say I will not make mention of Him nor speak any more in His name, then there is in my heart as it were a burning fire shut up in my bones, and I am weary with forbearing, and I cannot contain."[1] He was miserable if he spoke for God,

[1] xx. 9.

and he was more miserable if he kept silence. And so he went on with his work. He conquered his temptation. Every one is tempted to give up his work if it is difficult and disagreeable. All work for God is hard and brings many embarrassments and pains. There is a voice which keeps saying: "Give it up. What is the use of going on? What thanks do you get? What does your work amount to anyhow? Why not let somebody else do it? You have done more than your share." How subtle and persuasive that lower voice is. Thousands succumb to it. In every church there are men and women who started out to do some fine bit of work for God, but after a while they gave it up. They worked five years and then quit. They worked four years and that was enough. They worked three years and could not be induced to go on. They persevered one whole year and then were exhausted. Some of them had enough at the end of six months. They started out as a Sunday-school teacher, or as an officer of the Woman's Society or of the Men's Club or as a leader in the Y. P. S. C. E., but the work was disappointing, and the difficulties were many; and moreover they did not get any thanks for anything they did, and so they resigned. They gave up their job. They retired. They were tempted and they yielded.

In all our churches there are men and women who are not doing anything heroic or beautiful. They are not making any contribution to the higher life of mankind. This is their punishment: They are not in the Book of Life. Their names are not written on the walls of the City of God.

Jeremiah was like us in that he was a man of moods. Some one has said that our moods are lenses through which we see the world. Jeremiah was a man of many moods. He had his tearful moods. He has often been called the "Weeping Prophet." Never call him that. You have no right to call him a "Weeping Prophet." You say in justification that he wrote the Lamentations, but in saying that you are mistaken. He is not the author of the Lamentations. The tradition that he wrote them is false. The Lamentations were written by somebody else long after Jeremiah's day. He felt sometimes like crying. One day he poured out his soul in these passionate words: "O that my head were waters and mine eyes a fountain of tears, that I might weep day and night for the slain of the daughters of my people!" [2] There had been a battle and many of the boys of Jerusalem lay dead on the field of blood, and the heart of the prophet was torn with

[2] ix. 1.

[12]

anguish. In his grief he exclaimed: "Oh I wish I could cry my eyes out!" But that is no reason for calling him a "Weeping Prophet." Shelley once said: "I feel like a tired child, and could sit down and cry my life away." But no one calls Shelley a weeping poet. And no one calls Paul a weeping apostle, and yet the apostle wept again and again. He wept when he said "Good-by" to his dear friends at Miletus, and he tells the Philippians in his letter that while he writes about the disgraceful conduct of certain Christians the tears are running down his cheeks. Paul cried sometimes because he had a great tender heart, but he was not a weeping apostle. Jesus was not a weeping teacher. He wept in the cemetery at Bethany. He wept on the slope of Olivet when he looked upon Jerusalem and knew that the city was rushing on blindly to its doom. He wept in the Garden of Gethsemane. He no doubt wept at other times. How can a man with a tender heart live in a world like this and not weep now and then? But Jesus was not a weeping teacher, nor was Jeremiah a weeping prophet. He never sniveled or blubbered or whined. He was a strong, brave man, but sometimes his grief became uncontrollable and he burst into tears.

He had his disgusted moods. There were times when he wanted to get away from people.

He longed to get away from everybody. "Oh that I had in the wilderness a lodging place of wayfaring men; that I might leave my people, and go from them."[3] Or as we would say, "Oh, for a shack in the woods that I might be by myself for a year!" Why did he want to get away from people? They got on his nerves. He was sick of society and he longed for solitude. Why do we sometimes desire to get away from people? They get on our nerves. The conventionalities of society wear us out. The social entanglements bewilder and exhaust us. The social hypocrisies and shams disgust us, and we want to take to the woods. "Oh, for a lodge in the woods where I might hide myself forever!" Of course we do not mean it. We should soon get sick of the woods. There are too many bugs and worms there. We are soon glad to get back to people again. We cannot live without them. When we long to get away from them it is because our nerves are tired.

Sometimes Jeremiah became cynical, and in his cynical moods he spoke as foolishly as the rest of us. He was brought up in a little village about four miles from Jerusalem, and like all country boys he had rosy views of the glory and magnifi-

[3] ix. 2.

[14]

cence of the big city. When later on he moved
to Jerusalem he was disillusioned. The city was
not what he had imagined it was. When he came
into contact with the common people he discovered that nearly everybody tried to cheat him.
They were all sharpers and rogues. But he
excused them in his own mind saying, "Poor ignorant devils, they do not know any better. They
have never had a chance." He was sure that the
upper classes would be better. They had education
and would therefore know what a man ought to
be and do. But alas! when he got acquainted
with the upper classes, he discovered that they
were not a whit better than the people at the
bottom. They paid no attention to the laws of
God. They trampled on the primary principles
of morality. They were all liars. The city from
top to bottom was vile. And in the bitterness
of his heart he cried, "Run ye to and fro through
the streets of Jerusalem, and see now and know,
and seek in the broad places thereof, if ye can
find a man, if there be any that doeth justly, that
seeketh truth." [4]

He was in the mood in which Diogenes was
when he started out at noon with his lantern and
wandered up and down the streets of Athens.

[4] v. 1.

When some one asked him what he was looking for, he replied, "An honest man." Jeremiah was for a time a cynic. He said, "There is not an honest man in Jerusalem." He was as cynical as a Hebrew poet who said in his haste that all men are liars. We are all tempted to be cynics at times. We say in contempt, "They are all alike." Some people are disgusted with lawyers. They have had an unfortunate experience with one of them, or they have read about the shady transactions of several of them, and they say with sour disdain, "They are all alike." Some people are disgusted with doctors. They have had a sad experience with one of them, or they have read of the ignorance or rascality of several of them, and they say with a wry face, "They are all alike." Some people are disgusted with preachers. They say with contempt, "None of them know how to preach!" Some people are disgusted with church members. They have had dealings with a church member who is a hypocrite, and they say in derision, "They are all alike!" We never speak the truth when we are in a cynical mood. That is one thing to remember, a cynic cannot speak the truth. Some of you have probably said in a lower mood, "We are all alike." What nonsense that is. You know we are not all alike. Why tell yourself lies?

Jeremiah had his vindictive moods. In these moods he breathed forth vengeance. He had a host of enemies and they played on him dirty tricks. They lied about him and made fun of him and opposed him in everything he tried to do. He could stand a good deal, but he could not stand everything. Sometimes he hurled thunderbolts at his foes. One day a man by the name of Pashhur, an official of the temple, was so enraged by something that the prophet had been saying that he struck him, and being a man in authority he ordered that Jeremiah be placed in the stocks. He kept him there all that day in a most uncomfortable position, and every one who passed him pelted him with some stinging and insulting word. The poor man was kept there all night, and in the morning he was not in the best of humors. He let himself out against his enemies in language which almost frightens us. We had no idea that a prophet could or would say such terrible things. The imprecations of Jeremiah are something horrible.

One day when the fire in him was especially hot he asked God to do to his enemies almost every terrible thing he could think of. "Deliver up their children to the famine." That is, let their children starve to death. "And give them over to the power of the sword; and let their

Vindictive
18:21

Curses
18:21

[17]

wives become childless, and widows; and let their men be slain of death, and their young men smitten of the sword in battle." [5] And he ends his prayer by begging God never to forgive them, never to blot out their sin, and to deal with them only when he was in an angry mood.

Such language has caused Bible students no little perplexity. Some have tried to get around it by saying that Jeremiah never used such language. All such passages are interpolations. Somebody wrote such sentiments on the margin of the manuscript, and they worked their way into the body of the text. That is a sly way of getting rid of something you do not like. Others admit that the language is indeed that of the prophet, and they defend him in the use of it. They assert that it was all right for Jeremiah to feel and talk like that because he was a prophet and was inspired, but of course it would be all wrong for us to indulge in any such speech. That is an unfair way of getting around a moral difficulty. I think the wise thing for us to say is that it was all wrong for Jeremiah to talk after that fashion, and that he ought to have been ashamed of himself for giving way to such a spasm of vindictive frenzy. He was a good man but he sometimes allowed his lower self to master him. He was

[5] xviii. 21.

a great man but at times he was not great enough
to come up to our ideal of what a great man ought
to be. He was an Old Testament saint, and there
is a vast difference between an Old Testament
saint and a New Testament saint. When I was
in China I asked every one I met what he thought
of General Feng Yuhsiang. Do you think he is
a Christian? When I asked the question in Hong-
kong, the answer was, "He is an Old Testament
Christian." When I asked it in Shanghai I was
told he is an Old Testament Christian. When I
asked the question in Nanking the answer was,
"He is an Old Testament Christian." When I
asked it in Peking I received the same answer.
One would have supposed that all the missionaries
in China had gotten together and practiced their
part so as to be able to answer in unison, "He
is an Old Testament Christian." I understood
what they meant. They meant he was good as
far as he went. He was good up to the light he
had. He was sincere, but he was not up to par.
He was a Christian in spots, but he did not come
up to the ideal. He was an imperfect Christian,
a Christian not fully developed. Jeremiah was
a saint, but not a full-statured saint. He had in
him a vindictive spirit which I fear he never succeeded in conquering.

We Christians are under no obligation to defend vindictiveness even if it is exhibited in an Old Testament prophet. One day James and John said to Jesus, "Shall we call down fire and burn up the village of these churls who have insulted you?" He said, "No! Don't do it. Don't follow the example of Elijah." "Was he not a good man?" "Yes, good in some ways." "Was he not a great prophet?" "Yes, but you must not follow him at all points. You do not realize yet what spirit must dominate you. You have still the old vindictive spirit, the spirit which I have come to cast out. The Old Testament saints are not an example for you." The man who wrote the Letter to the Hebrews ran over a long list of the greatest and best men whom Israel had produced, and when he had completed the list he said, "Now these men are all around you and they will help you in various ways, but do not fix your eyes on them, fix your eyes on Jesus, let Him be your ideal!" Paul says that every bit of writing which has in it the Spirit of God is useful for several purposes, one is rebuke and another is correction. Samson is given a place in the Old Testament not as an example, but as a warning. He is the kind of man that young men ought not to become. The imprecations of Jeremiah are written for our admonition. That is the kind of spirit which we must endeavor to avoid.

Jeremiah sometimes talked like a fool. He was a wise man most of the time, but sometimes he was exceedingly foolish. His life was so full of suffering that sometimes he felt it was unendurable. Sorrow can become so intense and so long continued that one does not care to live any longer. Pain can become so awful that one wishes he had never been born. Jeremiah reached that point. At the end of the twentieth chapter is one of the saddest and bitterest paragraphs ever written. The prophet curses the day on which he was born. He invokes a curse on the man who carried word to his father that a new baby boy had come into the world. He denounces that man most furiously because he did not kill him the moment he was born. He wishes that he had died in his mother's womb. Foolish? Of course foolish. Insane? Yes, insane. The mind by trouble can become unhinged, and one can rave like a person who has lost his mind. Possibly some of us have at some dark hour in our life wished we were dead. Who knows but some one here has gone so deep into the abyss of grief as to wish he had never been born. If any of us has ever reached that depth of woe, or shall ever

reach it in the future, it may be some consolation
to know that one of the greatest and best men
whom God ever sent into this world trod the same
steep and thorny path. He was tempted in all
points even as we are.

Like us Jeremiah had his perplexities. There
were things he could not see through. He asked
God a lot of questions which God did not see fit
to answer. We err when we suppose that a
prophet knew everything, that he could see from
one end of a mystery to another. He carried like
the rest of us a mist in his mind and a fog in his
heart. One of the perplexities which puzzled him
most was the question, "Why do the wicked prosper?" "Righteous art thou, O Jehovah, when I
contend with thee, yet would I reason the cause
with thee; wherefore doth the way of the wicked
prosper? Wherefore are all they at ease that deal
very treacherously?" [6] He knows that God is just
and that his government is righteous, and yet all
around him he sees bad men successful. Wicked
men climb to high places, and scoundrels seem to
have nothing on their conscience. That is a perplexity which puzzles every man who thinks. It
is a perplexity twenty-five hundred years old, and
it was probably twenty-five hundred years old
when Jeremiah took hold of it. And twenty-five

---

[6] xii. 1.

hundred years from now men will be wrestling
with it still. It is a question which the mind will
never cease to ask. Why do the wicked prosper?
Why do liars get on so well? Why do dema-
gogues get elected to office? Why do rogues and
cheats enjoy popularity? Why does vice dress
in satin, and why does virtue go in rags? Why
is the way of the transgressor so often easy, and
why is the way of the good man so often hard?
Of course God is just. We all admit that. Of
course his government is perfect. We all concede
that. Why then do the wicked prosper? The
prophet asked the question, and God gave him
no answer. We ask the question, and God does
not tell us why. It is evident therefore that it is
not necessary for us to know. It is one of those
speculative questions which it is not needful to
answer. We can live useful and happy lives without an answer. We can postpone the question
until we arrive in the realm of light.

Another perplexity grew out of his own unhappy lot. "Why is my pain perpetual and my
wound incurable? Why am I so unhappy?
Why is my situation so galling? Why am I
ostracized, ignored and hated? I never can asso-
ciate with those who are happy or who are having
a good time. I am compelled to sit apart by
myself. I am lonely while others laugh and make

merry. Why do I suffer all the time?" That is a question which arises in every generation. Why are good men not happier than they are? If a man is devoted to the will of God why is he not honored, and why does his work not prosper? Why do good men suffer persecution? Why does God permit them to be misunderstood and maligned and slandered? Why does he allow them to go to prison, and why in many cases does he permit wicked men to put them to death? It is a piercing question, and there is no answer. It is an old question, old as the days of Jeremiah. It will puzzle the human intellect twenty-five hundred years from now.

A still more baffling perplexity was presented by human sin. He beheld the conduct of his nation with amazement. He could not understand why it persisted in sinning again and again. He could understand why a nation might slip back once or twice, but it was the perpetual backsliding which astonished and overwhelmed him. When a man stumbles he gets up. He does not keep on stumbling again and again. When a man wanders from the path he returns to it as soon as he discovers he has wandered from the right way. But in sinning it is different. Men stumble again and again. They keep on stumbling. There is no end to their stumbling. They wander from the path and wander farther and farther. They are like a horse on the battlefield. In its excitement it plunges ahead even though it plunges toward certain death. The migratory birds have in them an instinct which causes them to return to the point from which they started. But man does not seem to possess any such instinct. He flies away and does not come back.[7] Man does not seem to learn anything from the disastrous results of his sinning.

One day last Summer I saw a dog in a pitiable condition. He was lying on his side on the grass held down by a woman and a boy. A man kneeled at his head and was playing the part of a surgeon. The dog had had an interview with a hedgehog, and the dog's mouth was filled with quills. They had pierced his lip and his tongue and his gums. His mouth was a mass of blood. There must have been in his mouth several hundred quills. Every time the surgeon extracted a quill the dog winced, and I could hear him say, "Oh, how it hurts." I said to myself when I saw his suffering, "You will never look at a hedgehog again." But a man who was acquainted with the history of that dog told me that he had gone through the same experience before. This was not the first time the dog had had his mouth torn by the quills

---

[7] viii. 4-7.

of a hedgehog, and moreover the man assured me that the first hedgehog the dog might see in the future would cause him to go for it, bringing on him the same suffering again. I marveled at what I was told. It seemed incredible that so sensible a creature as a dog should be so inexcusably foolish. I pondered the phenomenon and I laid the problem before a friend of mine who possesses many kinds of wisdom. I asked him if it were really so that that dog would attack a hedgehog again? He assured me he would. Why, I inquired, should a dog be such a fool? He answered my question by asking another, "Why does a man make a fool of himself?" And so I have the problem still on my hands. It was the problem which Jeremiah had on his hands. All the prophets of the ages have had it on their hands, and no one has been able to give a better answer than the answer which Jeremiah gave: "The heart is deceitful above all things and desperately sick." [8] Jeremiah was a prophet but he was in all points as we are, and he was puzzled and baffled and bedeviled like ourselves.

All through his life Jeremiah was misunderstood and suspected and hated, but after his death men began to see him as he really was. His own generation did not appreciate him, but the gen-

[8] xvii. 9.

erations which followed saw him with eyes which discovered his greatness. As the centuries came and went men saw with increasing clearness that Jeremiah's work was not completed. The world still needs his fiery denunciations and passionate pleadings. If the world needs him, then surely he will come back again. It became a tradition among the Jews that Jeremiah would come back. In the hour of desperate need, men felt that Jeremiah was close at hand. In the second century before Christ when the Jews were in a life and death struggle with the Greeks, their leader, Judas Maccabaeus had a dream, and in his dream the majestic figure of Jeremiah rose before him, a glory in his face which he had never had on earth, and advancing toward the Jewish warrior the prophet handed him a golden sword. It is thus that the leaders of humanity draw courage from the hearts of heroes who have lived and suffered long ago.

There is a wonderful portrait in the Old Testament, the most remarkable one in that extraordinary volume. We call it the fifty-third chapter of Isaiah. In that chapter we have the portrait of the ideal man, the kind of man which an unknown prophet felt sure would some day come to redeem the world. Many Bible scholars are convinced that the painter of that portrait got his inspiration from the life and character of Jeremiah. When Jesus of Nazareth was in Galilee six hundred years after Jeremiah's death, he asked his disciples one day, "Who do men say that I am?" They replied, "Some say you are John the Baptist. Others say you are Elijah. Still others say you are Jeremiah." What a eulogy that was on the man of Anathoth! Men looked into the face of the Son of God and were so awestruck by the power and beauty which they saw there, that they could say nothing higher than, "You are Jeremiah."

good introduction

II

JEREMIAH THE THINKER

Who classes Jeremiah among the thinkers? It
has never occurred to many of us that he ever
did any thinking. The very idea that a prophet
should think is novel and surprising. When we
meditate on the world's great thinkers, our mind
turns to the philosophers. They are the thinkers.
They have nothing to do but to think. Everybody
knows that Socrates was a thinker, and so were
Plato and Aristotle and Thomas Aquinas and
Immanuel Kant and Hermann Lotze. Some of
us think first of all of the great scientific thinkers,
Kepler and Copernicus and Newton and Laplace,
and Clerk Maxwell and Faraday. Others of us
include the great political thinkers, men like
Cavour and Edmund Burke and Alexander
Hamilton. We are willing to include a few
essayists in our roll of the immortals, men like
Lord Bacon of England, and our own Ralph
Waldo Emerson. But most of us if asked to write
down the names of twenty of the world's greatest

thinkers, would never dream of including in the list the names of any of the Hebrew prophets.

The chief reason for this is probably because of the sharp distinction it is our custom to make between discovery and revelation. In the realm of religion we are in the habit of talking about revealed truth. It is revealed truth which is presented to us in the Bible. In all other books the truth has been discovered. The prophets were men to whom truth was revealed. God uncovered the truth. The prophet looked at it and reported what God had uncovered. The prophet overheard God's words and repeated them to his countrymen. The prophet did not think at all. It was God who did all the thinking. The prophet was an auditor, a spectator, and simply gave an account of what he saw and heard. That is the popular idea of a Hebrew prophet. He was an amanuensis, and his only labor was that of putting down on paper what he heard God say.

But in every realm other than religion, we know that a truth is discovered by human effort. In science and art men in search of truth must go on an arduous quest. They must dig and dig deep for every treasure which they obtain. As the poet says:

Not a truth has to art or to science been given,
But brows have ached for it, and souls toiled
and striven.

All who are familiar with the biographies of
great men know how terribly true this is. We
do not know much even yet, but what little we
do know has been acquired by an enormous expen-
diture of effort and toil. To ascertain the principles and laws of the physical creation, the scientists have paid an incalculable price. Scientists
must work for everything they get, whereas
prophets have the truth handed out to them!
This is the popular notion and it is totally mistaken.

Every groundless assumption works mischief
in many directions. The assumption that prophets
are not obliged to think like other men has led
many persons to conclude that thinking is not
an essential of religion. Religion is an emotional
and sentimental affair in the opinion of not a few.
To be religious one does not need to use his brain.
All that is essential is the use of his heart. Indeed
the less thinking the better. One ought to be
careful and not ask too many questions. If he
asks questions he may become an infidel. He
must not pry into things too deeply. If he does,
the consequences may be direful. He must not

criticize anything in the Bible or in the Creed or in the polity or program of the church, for this is sacrilegious. He must be on his guard against new ideas. New ideas are deadly to religion. He should keep aloof from all books which teach doctrines different from those on which he was brought up. These might upset his faith. He should refrain from the discussion of any question connected with religion. Religious controversy is scandalous. Men may perpetually discuss politics and science and art, but not religion. Religion is something which has been given to us and we must not think too much about it or we may lose it. In the realm of religion we must walk by faith and allow the intellect to take a vacation. This is the crude notion of many.

We need to remind ourselves again and again that we must love God with our mind. The Hebrew prophets loved Jehovah with all their mind. With everything that was within them they glorified his name. They were without exception great thinkers. They were full of questionings and at times full of doubts. They passed through fearful struggles and wrestled often through the night. They were free thinkers. They were not automatons or machines. Every one did his own thinking in his own way. Each one had his own vocabulary, his own favorite figures of speech, his own literary style, his own standpoint and his own points of emphasis. No two prophets were at all alike. How different Amos was from Hosea, and what a contrast there is between Isaiah and Jeremiah, and how widely these two differ from Ezekiel. They were all different because each one of them did his own thinking. God did not coerce them. They were not amanuenses. They were not phonographs. They were thinkers, free thinkers, and they worked their way to conclusions which were their own.

They were geniuses. We err when we think of them as ordinary men. There are critics of the Bible who place themselves above the Hebrew prophets. They will not admit that anybody living in Palestine twenty-five hundred years ago could have known any more than it is possible for everybody to know. It is ridiculous for any one to pooh-pooh the Hebrew prophets. The man who scoffs at genius is a man whose opinion is not worth heeding. Why should we deny genius when we have had so many indubitable exhibitions of it? There are chess geniuses—men who can play fifty games of chess at the same time and never once look at the board. You and I could not do that, if we tried for a hundred years. There are musical geniuses. Mozart was one of them, and we could not do in music what Mozart did if we worked five hundred years. There are mathematical geniuses, and we could not work out the differential calculus or a table of logarithms if we should be permitted to live a thousand years. There are literary geniuses, and what they did no one else can do. Shakespeare was such a genius. No other English baby has ever come into the world able to write a drama equal to Hamlet or Lear, and if the world should run on a million years, it is not at all certain that there will ever come a poet equal to the poet born in Stratford-on-Avon. Why should there not be spiritual geniuses, men dowered with special gifts of spiritual insight and comprehension, possessed of extraordinary faculties for apprehending spiritual processes and ascertaining spiritual laws? The Hebrew prophets are geniuses in the realm of the soul. We can afford to sit at their feet as pupils.

Because they were geniuses, they were prodigious workers. Some persons imagine that if a man is a genius he does not need to work at all. The fact is that only geniuses really know how to work. The average man does not know what work is. If a man whimpers and whines because he has to work, it is because he is mediocre. There is not much of him. The geniuses are all workers. Our most outstanding man of genius at the present hour is perhaps Thomas A. Edison. He is one of the world's most indefatigable workers. He is over eighty but he is still working as hard as he worked at forty. In the southern part of Florida he is spending this winter in a new form of work. He is trying to find out something. To find it out he is experimenting. He is willing to work weeks and months and years in order to find out something he wants to know. The Hebrew prophets were tireless workers, and therefore they found out things which have been a blessing to the whole world.

But if these prophets had to work for what they received, where does God come in? What had God to do with it? There are some who say he had nothing at all to do. This is an error. God met these men in their thinking. God is the great Thinker and he meets men who think. He thinks with them and helps them to think still more profoundly and more fruitfully. He met the prophets in their thinking and enlarged and enriched their thought. He met them in their work. He is the great worker, and he comes to men in their labor. He and men work together to carry out his plans. He meets them in their suffering. He is the great burden bearer, and he is with all who suffer. This is the central truth of the Christian religion that God is with us and in us, working out his own good pleasure. God was in the Hebrew prophets. He did wondrous things through them because they worked hard and suffered much. The writer of the Letter to the Hebrews stated the fact accurately when he wrote, "God of old time spoke unto the fathers in the prophets by divers portions and in divers manners."

The prophets had a way of saying, "Thus saith the Lord," a phrase which may easily mislead us. We may infer that the Lord spoke in an audible voice as one man speaks to another, and that the prophet listened to the voice and repeated what he heard. The expression is a pictorial way of describing a psychological process. The prophet thought and kept on thinking. He meditated, he brooded, he dreamed, until after a long time a conviction formed in his soul which was so deep-rooted and solid and vital, that he was certain he had come into possession of an idea of God, and in this assurance he went before his countrymen with a message, saying, "This is God's truth!" It was a word of the prophet, and at the same time it was a word of God. History has proved that words spoken by the prophets were indeed words of God. These men did really speak as they were moved by the Spirit of God.

That is why their words abide. The word of the Lord endures forever.

It is not easy to think of Jeremiah as a thinker. He has a bad reputation. He is called the "Weeping Prophet." It is easier to think of his tears than of his ideas. He was a man of passionate feeling. It is easier to think of his outbursts of passion than of his thoughts. He was a merciless critic of his city and nation. It is easier to think of the thunderbolts which he hurled at his generation than of his teachings. Many of us if asked to name the dominant ideas of Jeremiah, would be at a loss for an answer. We have never associated Jeremiah with ideas. In our Sunday-school days we were not instructed in the ideas of Jeremiah. Our teacher was more interested in the names of the kings who flourished in Jeremiah's day. We were told of Josiah, Jehoiakim and Jehoiachin and Zedekiah. We were given certain dates. Much emphasis in those days was placed on dates. Some of us can remember to this day the date 586, the year in which Jerusalem fell. The kings of Jeremiah and the dates of Jeremiah took so much space in our mind, that there was no room for the ideas of Jeremiah. It never occurred to us that he had any ideas. But dates and names of dead kings are not of much value in a world like this. They are as innutritious as sawdust. Ideas on the other hand are a form of food. They build up intellectual and moral muscle. We cannot get inspiration from a date, or comfort from the name of a dead king. It is ideas which stimulate us and make us strong. What a pity it is that we did not learn the ideas of Jeremiah in the days of our youth.

Not many of us, I fear, have read the Book of Jeremiah since we dropped out of the Sunday-school. Those of us who have read it occasionally have, I surmise, a hazy notion of its contents. We have come away from it with two or three episodes sticking in the mind. We have not come away with ideas. We remember that King Jehoiakim did not like Jeremiah, and cut his sermons into ribbons with a penknife and tossed the ribbons into the fire. We remember that, but we do not know what were the ideas written on the parchment which caused the king to cut it into pieces with his knife. We remember that Jeremiah was thrown into a cistern, and that a negro pulled him out; but it was his ideas which caused him to be thrown into the cistern, and we do not know what those ideas were. It is easy to read the Book of Jeremiah and come away empty-handed. Many professing Christians have never gotten anything worth while out of this wonderful book.

[38]

Something may be said on their behalf by way
of excuse. It must be confessed that for the
average reader Jeremiah is not an interesting
volume. It is repetitious and monotonous. Much
of it is gloomy. The literary style lacks distinction. There are few paragraphs which shine,
few sentences which linger in the ear like music.
There are no purple patches such as we find in
Isaiah. Isaiah is far more eloquent and more
rhetorical and more picturesque. Isaiah gives us
a vivid and unforgettable portrait of the Messiah,
but the portrait of the Messiah in Jeremiah is
tame and faded. Isaiah gives us a dazzling picture of the golden age. He sketches for us the
glory of a warless world. He tells us of the time
when nations are going to beat their swords into
plowshares and their spears into pruning hooks,
but nothing so splendid is pictured in the book
of Jeremiah. Moreover the contents of the book
are a hodgepodge. There is no chronological
sequence running through it. The chapters are
not in many cases, linked together, nor are even
the paragraphs in the same chapter. One paragraph tells you what happened in one reign, and
the next paragraph tells you what happened many
years later. The Bible scholars have had endless
trouble in working out the chronology, and they
are working at it still. Hardly any two of them

agree because they are compelled to work largely in the realm of conjecture.

Moreover Jeremiah is not a theologian. He is not a systematic thinker. He builds no system. He attempts no argument. He gives instruction on no religious doctrine. In the strict sense he is not a teacher. He gives no definitions. He draws no distinctions. He formulates no creed. He does not work out his theological or philosophical conceptions. He never attempts to instruct us in regard to any of his fundamental ideas. He believes in prayer, but he never says anything about it. You get his idea of prayer by a study of his prayers. He believes in the guilt and power of sin, but he gives no theory of sin. He does not speculate concerning its origin or its ultimate consequences. He never looks beyond this present world. You learn his idea of sin from his attitude to the social evils of his day. He has his idea of God but he never sets it forth as a reasoned doctrine. He never indulges in the pleasure of formulating propositions. You must get his conception of God from his outlook on the world. In short his ideas are not compact and solid entities which you can pick up like so many gems and enjoy the brilliance and flash of them.

His ideas are dissolved in the story of his life

and you must precipitate them by sending through
the book a current of thought. In order to get
much out of Jeremiah, you must think. You
must work. You must dig as for hidden treasures. You cannot do much without assistance.
It is futile to try to understand such a book without a commentary. You must have somebody to
guide your mental feet. Some one who has spent
years on the book and who knows all about the
historical environment which gave the book its
birth, must become your companion if you are to
be successful in grasping the message which the
book has to give. In these chapters I offer myself as a guide to encourage you in your studies.
My ambition is to stimulate your mind and induce you to make an honest effort to master the
cardinal ideas of this mighty Man of God.

Multitudes of intelligent and influential people
do not read the Bible. They do not read it because they get so little out of it. We cannot
expect people to read any book unless that book
gives them help. We get no help from the Bible
unless we master its ideas. It is a book of ideas.
It is its ideas which keep it alive. Jeremiah has
a place in the Bible solely because of his ideas.
If he had not been a great thinker, his name
would have lost its luster centuries ago. The
Bible holds its place among thinking people not

because of any theory of inspiration or because of arguments advanced by the theologians, but because of the power of its dominant ideas. Some persons are greatly alarmed by the concerted attacks which are now being made upon the Scriptures. They are fearful that the Bible may be overturned. There is no ground for these fears. The Bible is absolutely safe. If it rested upon something, its support might be taken away. But it rests upon no artificial or manufactured props. It is held up by its ideas, and until its ideas are discredited and proved false, it can never be overturned. Its ideas are words of life. They make alive. Men will live on them as long as the mind and heart endure.

Our age needs nothing so much as clear and constructive thinking. There seems to be a conspiracy on foot to keep us from thinking. Ours is the age of the automobile. We rush from place to place and glory in the rapidity of our movement, but we do not think while we are in motion. No thinking is done in an automobile. In the evening we go to the movies. If we are not moving ourselves we want to see other people in motion. Who was ever caught thinking at a moving-picture show? We have numberless magazines and papers, and these also keep many of us from thinking. We convert the mind into a rag bag into which we cram the odds and ends of other men's thoughts, and do no thinking of our own. What a lot of muddle-headed people there are! How few men and women there are to-day who can think straight. We are a spectacle to the nations because of our gullibility. There is no philosophy however stupid, and no hallucination however silly, and no scheme however wild, and no fad however ridiculous, which does not get a large following in this country. What is the matter with us? We do not think. We have lost the capacity for thinking. We are not educated to think. We have no time to think.

What is the supreme need of the Christian Church? More thinking. We do not think enough. Thousands of Christians are timid. Other thousands are cowardly. Other thousands are sloppy-minded. Some are afraid of philosophy and of science and of scholarship and of education and of evolution—in fact of everything, and all because they do not think. The prophets were thinkers. They denounced thoughtlessness as the deadliest of all curses. Isaiah in one of his great sermons cries, "The ox knows his owner, and the ass his master's crib, but my people do not know, my people do not consider, they do not use their mind, and because of this the church is impotent and the state is rotten." Jeremiah thunders against the same sin. A hundred years have gone since Isaiah's day, but the people are still staggering along in their old stupid ways. They say their prayers and offer sacrifices, but they do not think. They crowd the temple and ostensibly worship God, but they do not mix thought with their worship. They indulge in a disgusting form of cant. They say, "The Temple, The Temple! The Temple!" as though the temple could save a people who do not think. It is thinking that saves religion from degenerating into superstition. Without ideas religion is doomed. What is our chief sin? Lack of thought. How many of us really think in our religion? How often do we ask, "What is the meaning of this? Why am I doing this? What am I accomplishing by this? This church attendance? This praying? This celebrating the Lord's Supper? This church membership? What is it doing for me, for my city, for the world?"

We need Jeremiah. We need to keep step with a great thinker. If any of you should ask what help can we get from a Jew who lived twenty-five hundred years ago, the answer is that ideas are not antiquated because they are old. The Copernican system is old but it is up-to-date. The law of gravitation is old but it is not obsolescent. Galileo lived a long time ago, but the law of the pendulum has not been superseded. Archimedes lived centuries before Christ, but the physicist still uses the ideas which Archimedes gave to the world. We need the ideas of Jeremiah. He lived in the seventh century before Christ, and we live in the twentieth century after Christ, but we need his ideas. They are up-to-date. He lived in Jerusalem and we live in New York, but we need his ideas. They are fresh. Because God is the same, and the soul is the same, and truth never changes, Jeremiah can speak to our needs. The old passions are still working, and the old sins are still destroying. The heart still yearns and aspires. The soul still struggles and suffers. Life goes on, mysterious as ever. Death looks on, awful as of old. Perils threaten on the right hand and on the left. Destruction yawns in the distance. We need a thinker. We need Jeremiah.

Jeremiah lived in a dark age. We live also in a dark time. Superficial people think we are living in a bright time. They are deceived by the electricity. We have made the night to shine as the day, but the world still is dark. Something mightier than electricity is needed to banish the darkness. We are living in a somber time. Superficial people think we are living in a jolly time—an hilarious time. They think that because the bands are all playing Jazz. But when you get into a company of thoughtful people you find they are all serious, sober, and some of them somber because we have released forces, mighty forces, which unless controlled, will tear us to pieces. No one knows what the forces of civilization will do with us before they get done with us. The problems are vexatious and complex and baffling, some of them appalling, and others apparently insoluble. We need a thinker. We need Jeremiah. We need to see the stars by which he guided his course across a tempestuous sea. He carried a heavy burden, and our burden is by no means light. We need to find our way to the source of strength which he discovered. We need to sit at his feet and let him tell us the secret of his victory.

III

RELIGION IS AN AFFAIR OF THE HEART

Feb 24

17:10

One of the key sentences of the Book of Jeremiah is that recorded in the tenth verse of the seventeenth chapter: "I the Lord search the heart, I try the reins." Through that sentence let us work our way into the core of the prophet's message. It is easy to read the book without getting one's eye on this sentence, and even after the eye has found it, its meaning is not readily discerned. One can imagine the puzzled look of a bright boy who comes upon this sentence for the first time. I can hear him saying, "Mother, why does God try the reins?" The mother would explain to the boy that words are used in different senses. In one sentence a word may mean one thing, whereas in another sentence it may mean something altogether different. The English language has over four hundred thousand words, but it has not words enough to go round. It is necessary to use the same word to express a half

[47]

dozen or even a dozen different meanings. The only reins which the boy knows anything about, are the straps attached to a bridle with which a man guides and controls his horse.

But reins in this sentence in Jeremiah means "kidneys." It is a word which has come to us from the Latin by way of the old French, and its meaning in French and Latin is "kidneys." The sentence translated into plain English would read, "I the Lord search the heart, I try the kidneys." But that puzzles the boy more than ever. He asks, "Mother, why does God try the kidneys?" The chances are that at this point the mother will ask to be excused and she will suggest that the boy go to the Sunday-school teacher for fuller information. If the teacher has been instructed, he or she will explain to the boy that the central part of the human body is the most sensitive and vital part. In that quarter are placed several highly important organs, among them the kidneys. The region around the kidneys is called the "loins," and as everybody knows the word "loins" is of frequent occurrence in the Scriptures. Sometimes the word "loins" is dropped for the word "kidneys." The Jews localized the emotions and affections in the loins or kidneys. We localize them higher up. We locate them in the heart. It seems natural to us to localize them in

[48]

the heart, because we have always done it. It seemed natural to the Jews to localize them in the kidneys because their ancestors had always done it. Their way was just as sensible as ours. Their way seems ridiculous to us simply because we are not accustomed to it. There is no rational reason why we should localize the emotions and affections in the heart. The physical organ which we call the "heart" has no feeling in it. We never know we have a heart until its action becomes abnormal, and we never know we have kidneys until they become diseased. In neither the kidneys nor the heart are there any emotions or affections.

We use "heart" as a figure of speech, and the Jews used "reins" or "kidneys" in the same way. Jewish poets could write poetry about the kidneys. Our poets cannot. Job cries out, "He cleaveth my reins asunder!" [1] That is the Jewish way of saying, "He breaks my heart." The Psalmist says, "Thou hast possessed my reins." [2] That is the Jewish way of saying, "Thou hast taken possession of my heart." Whenever, therefore, you find the word "reins" in the Bible, rub it out and substitute the word "heart." The sentence in Jeremiah therefore runs, "I the Lord search the heart, I try the heart."

[1] xvi. 13.
[2] cxxxix. 13.

[49]

But we have not gotten the sentence correct yet. The prophet does not say in Hebrew, "I search the heart, I try the heart." He uses two different Hebrew words in that sentence, and they do not mean the same thing. He uses a word often translated by the word "heart," but that Hebrew word has a wider meaning than our English word "heart." By "heart" the Hebrew meant the organ of purpose and reason and thought, and not simply the organ of feeling. Our Lord was speaking like a Jew when he said one day, "Out of the heart proceed evil thoughts." We would say "out of the mind." Very often in the Bible the word "heart" means mind, and should be so translated. In this sentence the word "heart" means mind, and when correctly rendered it reads, "I the Lord search the mind, I try the heart."

When you consult the Revised Version of the Bible, you find that is the way this sentence stands. The Revisers have given us the correct translation. This is a fresh reminder of the fact that every Christian ought to own a copy of the Revised Version of the Bible. If you want melodious English, then the King James' Version is preferable to all others, but if you want to understand the ideas of the Hebrew writers, you cannot get on without the Revised Version. This then is the sentence with which we now have to do, "I Jehovah search the mind, I try the heart." In other words, "I take account of a man's thoughts and affections."

It is a regrettable fact that every English translation of the Bible gives us in various ways a false impression. This constant repetition of the word "heart" in our English Bible misleads us. It gives religion a super-emotional complexion. For we always read into the word "heart" the meaning adopted by popular English usage. Most persons consequently think that religion is primarily an emotional thing. The intellect is ruled out. You have heard people say, "I am not very religious. I have never had any of those feelings which you read about in the books." Or you have heard some one say, "Mr. A. is very religious. He overflows with emotion." Or you have often heard it said, "Women are more religious than men. They have so much more feeling!" The result is that many persons measure their religious condition by the state of their feeling. If they feel good, they think they are good. If they feel bad, they think they are bad. But all such deductions are unsound. One can feel good and be bad, and one can feel bad and be good. You cannot determine your standing before God by consulting your feelings.

The most unfortunate outcome of this false reading of the Bible is the prevalent opinion that to be religious it is not necessary to think. You can be a good Christian and not think at all. Indeed the notion is abroad that it is dangerous to think in the realm of religion. You have got to think in business. You go to the dogs in business if you do not think, and think hard. You have got to think in science. You get nowhere if you do not think. But in religion you must be careful. You must not think too much. You must not think deeply. If you think too deeply you may become an infidel." Religion is doomed as soon as men cease to think. Superstition yawns and swallows them up. The Bible does not make its appeal primarily to the emotions. Its primary and deepest appeal is always to the intellect, the reason, the mind. The Old Testament expresses its most thrilling appeal in the great exhortation put into the mouth of God: "Come now let us reason together, let us argue this matter out, let us think this subject through, and let us see if we cannot arrive at some rational and satisfactory conclusion." In the New Testament, our Lord is always asking: "How do you think? What do you think? Why do ye not of yourselves judge what is right?" You cannot be a good Christian unless you think.

Religion according to Jeremiah, is an affair of the heart. By "heart" I mean what the Bible means, an affair of the interior life, of the soul, of the innermost chamber of personality. There has always been a tendency to make religion something external, formal, ritualistic. The human race has always been haunted and plagued by the delusion that God is angry with men, angry because of their sins, and that he must be appeased by making him presents. You must give him something to placate him. You must offer him a gift to induce him to be friendly. And so through the ages, men have been giving God things, sometimes a sheep or a goat or a bullock, sometimes a sheaf of grain or a pot of oil or a basket of flowers, or sometimes they have even sacrificed their eldest sons, thinking that in this way God would come round and show his favor. That was the delusion which held sway through thousands of years, and the delusion still prevails in many parts of the world.

But nineteen hundred years ago in Palestine there lived a man who broke away from this age-long tradition. He believed that God does not ask or expect material gifts. What he wants is love. All he asks is the heart, the mind, a man's own self. This idea soon spread and a Jew by the name of Paul gave it classic expression in an address recorded in the Book of the Acts. Paul declared boldly that God does not dwell in temples made with hands, he dwells in the heart. He does not want things made with the hands, he wants the heart. He does not need any material thing for he owns everything, all he wants is the fellowship of the heart. That idea went out into all parts of the world. A new religion had taken its place in human history—Christianity.

But by and by the old idea crept into this new religion. Men began to fall back into the old pagan notion, that in order to please God you must do something. God is angry and you must win him by doing things. You must go to mass. The mass is a bloodless sacrifice, and you must see it offered. You must go to confession. You must perform penances. You must go on pilgrimages. You must invoke the saints. Unless you do all these things you cannot enjoy the favor of God.

Through a thousand years the church gave itself up more and more to this pagan idea. Christianity became paganized, and the world became increasingly dark. In the earlier sixteenth century, a man in Europe cried aloud, "Let us go back to the New Testament. Let us embrace the apostolic idea of religion. Let us believe that we are saved not by anything we do, but simply by coming into fellowship with God." The idea traveled out in all directions. A new church was formed, the Protestant Church, a group of Christians who protested against the pagan idea that you must appease God by the things you do. The new church exhibited wonderful power, and human hearts were glad again with the same joy which the Apostles knew. But by and by the old pagan idea crept in again. It seems well-nigh impossible to keep it out. It found entrance into Protestantism and men began to think again that religion is a matter of good works. You must read the Bible, you must sign a creed, you must go to church. If you do not do these things you are lost. And so little by little it became generally believed that religion is a matter of tradition and custom. There are certain traditions which you must cling to, and there are certain customs which must never be given up, for if you surrender either the traditions or the customs, God will have no mercy on you.

But religion is a matter primarily neither of tradition nor of custom. It is an affair of the heart. Twenty-five hundred years ago, Jeremiah proclaimed that glorious message, and the world has not learned it yet. We are still in need of Jeremiah.

How did Jeremiah find it out? The old answer was, "God revealed it to him." That is a correct answer, but it is not intelligible. We want to know how God revealed it to him. We find this out by a careful study of the book which tells the story of his life. God revealed it to him through his experiences and observations. Jeremiah used his eyes and his head. By a faithful and long-continued use of these he found out something which the world needed desperately to know. The prophet was a keen observer. He watched men. He studied them. He saw them coming to the temple. He observed them in their worship. He listened to their songs and prayers. He took note of their sacrifices. All this he carefully took in, and he also noticed that this temple worship seemed to have no influence on the conduct of the men who engaged in it. They were the same men after worship that they were before. They said their prayers, but their prayers did not change their disposition. They sang their songs, but their songs did not alter their temper. Their religion left no mark upon their conduct. And so the conviction grew upon Jeremiah, that true religion is not external. It is an affair of the heart. He saw that. He saw it because he used his eyes and put his mind behind his eyes.

He also watched his nation. In his day there occurred a national reformation—the greatest reformation which Israel had ever known. The question at issue in the reformation was in regard to the place or places in which sacrifices could be offered. There were many sanctuaries located in different parts of the land. Shrines had been set up on many hilltops throughout Judea. At these local altars the people were in the habit of carrying on their worship. But in the course of time, many abuses crept in. The old Canaanitish superstitions emerged. Irregularities sometimes of a shameful character were tolerated, and at last a group of the most spiritually-minded leaders in Jerusalem became convinced that to conserve the ethical values of religion, it was necessary to cut off these local shrines and confine all offering of sacrifices to the temple in Jerusalem. That was the conclusion of the religious leaders, and the king acted on their recommendation. He commanded that all the local sanctuaries should be destroyed, and that every Jew must offer his sacrifice in Jerusalem. The reformation was universal and carried out with drastic thoroughness. But Jeremiah noticed that the reformation did not reform the people. They remained after

[57]

the reformation what they were before. The conviction deepened in him that religion is not an affair of locality, but an affair of the heart. No matter where a man may worship, he worships in vain if he does not worship with his heart.

He watched also his own heart. He enjoyed fellowship with God. God was his friend, and he conversed with him day by day. He saw his nation was doomed. He realized that the policy of its political rulers would bring it to destruction. He foresaw that the city would be captured, the temple would be burned, the people carried into captivity, but he felt sure that all these calamities would not break down his own fellowship with God. They would not destroy his religion. Nothing external can destroy a man's religion, for religion is an affair of the heart. He saw this because he used his eyes and his mind. God revealed this to him because he was willing to think and think hard.

And so he was driven by his thinking to the most radical and amazing conclusions. He became convinced that animal sacrifices are not essential to religion. Imagine a Jew of the seventh century before Christ arriving at such a conclusion. He boldly asserted [3] that when

---
[3] vii. 22.

[58]

God led the Israelites out of Egypt he said
nothing to them about burnt offerings or sacrifices.
All he asked of them was obedience. "If you
obey me I will be your God, and you shall be my
people." The Israelites in those early years enjoyed the manifest favor of God without any
animal sacrifices whatever, and therefore it is
certain that animal sacrifices are not essential to
religion. What a courageous man this is!

Not even the ark is necessary.[4] Every
pious Jew supposed it was. The ark was sacred.
It guaranteed the divine presence. The Jews had
always felt that without the ark they would be
undone. But Jeremiah declares that the ark is
not at all necessary. The time will come, he says,
when men will forget all about the ark. It will
slip entirely out of their mind. It will vanish
and they will not miss it. What a bold man this
is!

Not even the Temple is necessary. The Jews
were proud of their temple. They idolized it.
They were always saying to one another, "The
Temple of Jehovah, the Temple of Jehovah, the
Temple of Jehovah!" "But the Temple of
Jehovah will never save anybody," said Jeremiah.
You may call a building the Temple of Jehovah,
and yet Jehovah may have nothing to do with it.

[4] iii. 16.

[59]

A temple may become a cave of robbers[5] and that is what it really is if men with dishonest hearts are worshiping within its walls. What a daring man this is!

Even the Tables of the Law are not indispensable to religion. The Jews supposed they were. They were believed to have been engraved by the finger of the Almighty. They were counted the most precious treasure of the Israelitish people. They were kept in the ark, and the ark was kept in the Holy of Holies, but not even these sacred stones, the Prophet asserts, are essential to religion. Unless the law is written on the heart it is of no value to a man or a nation. What an audacious man this is!

The City of Jerusalem is not essential to the prosperity of religion. Every Jew thought it was. To him Jerusalem was the City of the Great King. Jerusalem was dear above all other cities to the heart of God. Jerusalem was the center from which the law of God was to be radiated into the whole world. Jerusalem was under God's special protection. No foe could ever capture it. No calamity could ever overwhelm it. The great Prophet Isaiah a hundred years before had declared that Zion was inviolable, and that no Pagan King, no matter how mighty, could ever break

[5] vii. 11.

[60]

down its gates. But Jeremiah asserts that Jerusalem can be taken and will be taken. Its walls
will be battered down, its palaces will be burned,
its temple will go up in smoke, the Holy of
Holies will be reduced to ashes, but religion will
not be extinguished, because religion is an affair
of the heart. What a wild radical this man is!

Nor is the Jewish nation essential to the sur-
vival of true religion. Every devout Jew supposed
it was. The people had been trained through
centuries to look upon themselves as God's chosen
people. They were the instrument in God's hand
for executing his purpose in the world. He had
made them innumerable promises and not a promise would be broken. Through the Jewish nation
salvation was to come to all mankind. The nation
therefore was indestructible. Without it God
could not do his work. But Jeremiah declares
that the nation will be destroyed, its political
machinery will be broken to bits, its country will
be taken from it, its independence will be lost, it
will cease to be called a nation among the nations
of the earth. What a reckless man this is. Oh,
the audacity of him!

He does not hesitate to say that true religion
cannot be linked indissolubly with any tradition
or any custom or any institution or any city or
any nation or any people. Religion is an affair of

the heart, and therefore cannot be obliterated. God is indestructible, and so also is the soul, and so long as God and the soul endure, religion can never be destroyed. This is the conviction of Jeremiah. In his company you are in the presence of one of the greatest men God ever sent into this world.

Our age is in need of Jeremiah. We need some one to make clear to us the essentials of religion. We have lost our way in a wilderness of superficial and inconsequential things. Many good people are uneasy, some of them are sorely troubled, and a few of them are in keen distress. They are worried and dejected because so many things are being shaken and other things are losing their grip upon the modern mind. The old stories in the Book of Genesis are being given up, not solely by liberals and radicals, but by good old-fashioned and sensible Christians, pillars in the Church of Christ. The story of the Creation of man and the story of the fall, these have been accepted as God's truth for centuries, and upon these it has been commonly supposed that Paul built his theology, and if these foundations are removed, what is going to become of the Christian religion? I do not wonder that many persons are bewildered.

Hallowed customs are being surrendered.

[62]

The old fashioned ways are disappearing

Some are going and others have already gone.
The old custom of teaching the children the
catechism and having the pastor examine them on
his round from home to home—that went long
ago. The custom of family worship is going. It
has already gone from a majority even of our
most religious homes. The practice of attending
two services on Sunday is going. Many churches
have discontinued the second service altogether.
It seems to many that religion itself is going.
Why then should we marvel that many of the
saints are in distress?

But we should remind ourselves that no new
thing is happening. Religion to its contemporaries has always seemed to be going. So it seemed
to the devout Jews of the first century. They
had grown up to think of religion in connection
with the altar and the sacrifices and the priesthood and the temple. Without these, religion
could not get on. These were indispensable to
the true Church of God.

But a new interpretation of religion arrived,
and all these things considered indispensable were
forthwith discarded. The altar was abandoned,
the sacrifices ceased, there was no longer any of-
ficiating priesthood, and religious people met for
worship not in a temple but in private homes. And
yet religion went on, and not only went on but went

up. Religion began to move on a higher level. It is incontestable that Christianity moves on a higher level than did ancient Judaism. We have tried the experiment through nineteen hundred years and no one can deny that religion in the form of Christianity is more vigorous and powerful than religion in the form of Judaism. The religion of Jesus is superior to the religion of Moses.

In the sixteenth century the devout Roman Catholics felt that Christianity was going when Protestants gave up the Pope and the Mass and the Confessional and pilgrimages and the Virgin Mary. Every Catholic had been taught from babyhood that these things were absolutely essential. Without them there would be nothing of value left. How can you have a church—a true church of Christ—without a Pope and the Mass and the Confessional and Purgatory and the Virgin Mary? This was the query born in the Roman Catholic heart. Protestantism swept all these away, and the Roman Catholic was certain that Christianity in Protestant countries was doomed. But Christianity went on, and not only on but up. Christianity in Protestantism began to move on a higher level. The experiment has been tried for four hundred years and it has been demonstrated that religion is more vital and powerful and beneficial in its Protestant form than in its Roman

Catholic form. Just a look at the map of the world is sufficient to prove that!

And now in the twentieth century we have come to another crisis. Things long counted indispensable are being left behind. The authority of the Bible is being questioned. In many quarters it is being openly repudiated. We can now sympathize with the Roman Catholics of four hundred years ago. They were thrown into a panic by the denial of the authority of the church. What can you do, they asked, without an infallible authority? The Protestant replied, "We have an authority and it is an infallible authority. Here it is—the Bible." But now the authority of the Bible is denied, and what can the Protestant say? He can say, "We do not need any external authority. The seat of authority lies within. Religion is an affair of the heart, and cannot be linked forever with any institution, whether church or book, which lies outside of itself. Christianity is safe so long as we have the human heart."

As for the discarding of certain practices, let us not be needlessly alarmed. There are different types of piety, and religion delights in creating new forms of expression. The monks of the Middle Ages were in many cases good men. I am very fond of them. Their idea of goodness was that to be highly good one must cut loose entirely from society and go into a monastery and spend the days in prayer and penitential exercises. A man must take the vows of celibacy and poverty and obedience in order to win the highest approbation of God. That was the universal belief in the thirteenth century. But in the seventeenth century, another group of good men arrived—the Puritans. They believed that a good man ought to marry, and build a home, and bring up children, and go into business, and make money, and use his money in building hospitals and schools, and do his utmost to make men healthy and happy and useful. The Puritans were just as religious as the monks, but the monks did not think so. The monks thought the Puritans were going straight to the devil. The monks were mistaken. The Puritans were simply moving closer to God. Their piety had taken a different form.

We twentieth-century people are religious in a still different way. We have discarded most of the customs of the Puritans. We do not like long prayers. The long prayer in the seventeenth century was thirty minutes long, sometimes forty. Now it is less than ten, sometimes only five. We have given up the Puritan idea of the Sabbath. It is to us the Lord's Day, and we believe it was made for man. The Puritans allowed themselves the privilege of doing hardly anything on the Lord's Day beyond reading the Bible and going to church. We claim the right to do anything on the Lord's Day, which does not injure us or anybody else. We do not read the Bible as the Puritans read it. They began with Genesis and read straight on until they reached the last page of Revelation. We pick out the books and the chapters which help us most. We do not consider it to be our duty to read every paragraph of every book in the Sacred Volume.

We do not do many of the things which the Puritans felt God wanted all men to do, but we are nevertheless religious. We show our religion in new ways. We organize Y. M. C. A.'s and Y. W. C. A.'s and Y. P. S. C. E.'s and Men's Leagues and Women's Clubs and Boy Scouts and Girl Scouts, and a hundred different kinds of societies and organizations for social service and community uplift. We are as religious as the Puritans, but we show our piety in a new fashion. Religion is an affair of the heart, and each generation has the right to be religious in its own way.

Jesus was an admirer of Jeremiah. We ought to reverence his book because Jesus loved it so. Jesus read it again and again. Jesus got help out of it. This man of the seventh century helped Jesus do his work. Sometimes he quoted

[67]

Jeremiah's exact words. One day in the temple Jesus saw a crowd of hucksters and money-changers marring the worship by their worldly clatter, and at once the words of Jeremiah leaped to his lips, "This temple was built to be a house of prayer, but you have made it a cave of robbers."

Jesus adopted Jeremiah's idea of religion when he told the woman of Samaria that God is spirit, and that they who worship him must worship him in spirit and truth, he was giving expression to Jeremiah's conception. When he told the Pharisees that it is not what goes into a man's mouth, but what comes out of his heart that really matters, he was following again Jeremiah. When he told men that before they engaged in worship, they must get their heart right with their brother, he expressed an idea announced by Jeremiah six hundred years before. Like Jeremiah, Jesus could not be dismayed by any external calamity however great. He saw in his mind's eye the destruction of Jerusalem, the burning of the temple, the annihilation of the Holy of Holies and the slaughter and scattering of the people, but he never gave up hope. "Do not be afraid, little flock, my father is going to give you the kingdom." So he said under a sky without a star. The Kingdom of God is going to be established on this earth. "Go therefore and disciple the nations, and I will be with you always." No wonder that some of the people who heard him speak, said one to the other, "This is Jeremiah!" They caught in his preaching the note that had sounded clear and strong in the speech of the man of Anathoth. Jesus showed his supreme confidence in Jeremiah's fundamental idea, when he founded his church on an ordinary man who had nothing to commend him beyond the fact that his heart was in communion with God.

IV

THE INDIVIDUAL IS THE KEY OF THE WORLD PROBLEM

To the thoughtful mind the world is a problem. By world I mean the world of men and women, the world of human society, a wonderfully intricate and complicated organism, shot through with inflammable stuff and explosive forces, and pregnant with a thousand possible catastrophies. The problem is how to keep society from degenerating, disintegrating, rotting. Jesus of Nazareth, the man who understood the world better than any other man who has ever lived in it said that the world needs two things, light and salt— light to keep it from tumbling into a ditch, and salt to save it from putrefaction.

The rise and fall of empires has long been a subject for the contemplation of historians. A tragic theme it is. The dissolution of nations, the disappearance of races, this is a pathetic and doleful tale. Lord Byron read history, and at the end of his reading, this is what he wrote:

[70]

First Freedom and then Glory—when that fails,
Wealth, vice, corruption—barbarism at last.
And history with all her volumes vast,
Hath but one page.

Will our civilization go down? We do not know. We know that other civilizations have vanished. The civilization of Assurbanipal, of Nebuchadnezzar, of Rameses II., of Cyrus the Great, of Pericles, of the Antonines, of the Goths and the Saracens and the Aztecs—all these arose, flourished and dissolved. Will ours also go down? We only know it cannot go on as it is. It is too dishonest. Society is honeycombed with hypocrisies and shams and lies. It cannot go on indefinitely. It is too unbrotherly. The men at the top are too indifferent to the way in which the men at the bottom are obliged to live. Races are too snobbish in their attitude to one another, and classes are too cruel in their treatment of one another. It cannot go on. It is too stupid. Great Britain and France and the United States are spending hundreds of millions of dollars on the armies and navies, notwithstanding they have just come out of a war loaded down with debt. Here is stupidity in its densest and deadliest form. It cannot go on. Unless our civilization is improved, it is doomed.

What can be done? One reply is that nothing

can be done but to pull it down, rip it up, blow
it to atoms, and make room for something different. That is what the Bolshevists say, and the
Communists and the Syndicalists and the Anarch-
ists—groups of alert and determined men who are
working in every country to disseminate the philosophy of destruction.

The majority of men, however, are not concerned with the problem at all. They do not
want to be bothered with it. They go on eating
and drinking, marrying and giving in marriage,
making money and spending it, willing that civilization should drift on God only knows whither.

But there are groups of noble-minded men in
every country who believe that humanity can be
reformed, the world can be reshaped if only
resolute men once get their hands on it. But these
men are not agreed in regard to what must be
done. The reformation cannot come—so it seems
—through the state or the church or the school
or the press. All these agencies seem to be impotent, and labor spent on them is apparently futile.
We have no instrument at hand with which we
can reform the world. Where shall we seek for
a solution for the world problem? Where shall
we find the key which will unlock the closed door?
Let us consult the Prophet Jeremiah and see what
suggestion he has to offer.

Do you ever use a Concordance? You can learn things from a Concordance which you can learn from no other book. You can learn, for instance, in a moment that the word "heart" occurs more frequently in the book of Jeremiah than in any other book in the Bible except Proverbs and the Psalter. It occurs so frequently in the Psalter because the Psalms were largely written by poets who were powerfully influenced by Jeremiah. The word occurs several scores of times in the Book of Jeremiah, because religion in him has for the first time become intimate and personal, inward and individualistic.

In the earlier stages of Hebrew development religion was tribal. There were several Semitic tribes inhabiting Western Asia, and each tribe had its own God. There was a God of the Ammonites and a God of the Canaanites and a God of the Edomites and a God of the Midianites and a God of the Moabites and a God of the Philistines, and also a God of the Jews. This last God was named "Jehovah." He looked after his people. He rewarded them when they did well, he punished them when they did wrong. He gave the tribe prosperity in peace and victory in war. By and by the twelve tribes of the Jews were amalgamated into a nation and their religion became a national religion. Church and State were united. The individual had no religious or political existence apart from the nation. No Jew had any rights or responsibilities as a human being. His rights and responsibilities belonged to him solely as a member of the Hebrew nation. The nation was the religious unit, and throughout the Old Testament, the nation is spoken of as though it were an individual. Sometimes it is called God's "wife." He is the husband. The nation and God have been married. Lack of loyalty to God is adultery. Sometimes the nation is God's "Son." Such it was to Hosea when he wrote, "Out of Egypt have I called my Son." Sometimes it is called "God's servant." Such it was to Isaiah. Through hundreds of years the religious thinking of the Jews was done in nationalistic terms. God is the God of Jacob. Jacob was the name of the nation. God is the God of Israel. That was another name for the nation.

But in the eighth century a terrible thing happened. Ten of the twelve tribes of the nation were carried off into captivity by the Monarch of Assyria, and they never came back again. In the sixth century something still more terrible occurred, the other two tribes were carried off into captivity by the Monarch of Babylon. This time Jerusalem was destroyed, the Temple was burned, the nation was blotted out. A crisis had come in the history of the human race.

In this dark hour there appeared a man—Jeremiah was his name—who caught an idea which has left its mark on all subsequent generations. This man got his eyes on the individual. In the destruction of Jewish institutions, there was one object which remained, the individual man. Society was dissolved into its primordial elements, and out of the chaos there emerged a new hero— the one man. All the political and ecclesiastical machinery went up in smoke, and through the black clouds of rolling vapor, Jeremiah caught glimpses of the glory of the individual soul. For the first time he came to realize the dimensions of human personality. He was driven in on himself. He came into a fuller knowledge of himself. All the bonds by which he was bound to other men were broken. The ties of fellowship between him and the king and between him and the princes and the prophets and the priests and the people, all were dissolved. He had no wife or children. He dwelt in isolation. He lived in an awful solitude. And in this solitude he came to know as no man before him had ever known, the depth of the heart, the reach of the mind, the strength of the spirit, the worth and dignity of the soul. He saw for the first time that the only power which can break the force of inherited tradition, is the power of a man linked with God. The only influence which can overcome a false public opinion is the influence of a man who is true to God. The only way to check the lurch of the world toward the abyss is to throw against it the inflexible determination of a consecrated man.

NB

And thus did a new conception of the power of the one man come into the world. A new sense of personal responsibility was born. A fresh sacredness came into the word "duty." From this time onward religion is going to revolve round the dignity and immeasurable worth of the individual soul. Henceforth men are to be taught that the individual is the key of the world problem.

NB,

Let us note how this idea is expressed in the Book of Jeremiah. It comes and goes like a ghost, it flits to and fro, it appears and disappears, sometimes it is so subtle it will escape you unless your eyes are keen. You catch a foreshadowing of it in the fifth chapter. The prophet says that God told him to go through the streets of Jerusalem and try to find an honest man. God says that if he can find one honest man, the city shall be pardoned. There was an old tradition among the Jews that God long ago had declared that

ch. 5

[76]

he would save a certain city if ten righteous men could be found in it. But Jeremiah makes a great advance on the earlier idea. He sees that even ten men are not essential. There is hope for a city if in that city there lives one man willing to stand up for the truth!

In the seventeenth chapter you come to the same idea expressed in a picturesque form. "Blessed is the man that trusteth in the Lord, and whose hope the Lord is. For he shall be as a tree planted by the waters, and that spreadeth out its roots by the river, and shall not fear when heat cometh, but its leaf shall be green; and shall not be careful in the year of drought, neither shall cease from yielding fruit." That strikes a new note in the history of religion. Long afterwards a poet, whose name we do not know, seized upon this idea of Jeremiah and worked it out into the exquisite literary gem which is known to us as the First Psalm. It is an interesting fact that when a group of Jewish editors got together to pick out of Hebrew literature a hundred and fifty of the best poems, they said to one another, "Let us place on the front page of our volume the picture of a good man imaged by Jeremiah under the likeness of a tree."

In the thirty-first chapter we find the same idea expressed in relation to sin. "In those days they shall say no more, the fathers have eaten sour grapes, and the children's teeth are set on edge." The Jews had become fatalists. They had come to feel the tremendous force of heredity so keenly that they had lost the sense of personal responsibility. The generation preceding them had sinned and they were forced to pay the penalty for their ancestors' transgression. There was no escape. They were all in the same boat. No matter what they did or did not do, they were doomed.

It became an adage among them that the fathers had eaten sour grapes, with the result that the children's teeth were set on edge. Jeremiah picks up the adage and repudiates it. He says, "That is not so! Men are not punished for the sins of others. Every one shall die for his own iniquity; every man that eateth the sour grapes, his teeth shall be set on edge." In that declaration you behold a mighty stride forward in the progress of religious thought. Here is a man who has come to see that no one can be punished for any sin but his own. Under the government of God no man is ever punished for another man's misdoings. Every man is punished for his own sin and for his own sin only. Evil consequences, of course, flow down over the innocent. We often suffer from the sins of others, but our suffering is not punishment. If I happen to be passing through the street where two men are fighting with revolvers, I may be struck by a flying bullet, but that would not be punishment. I would suffer for the sin of another, but I should not be punished. Every man stands on his feet before the judgment seat of God and answers for the sins committed in his own body. Jeremiah is right. "Every one shall die for his own iniquity; every man that eateth the sour grapes, his teeth shall be set on edge." The individual is responsible for his own sin.

In the third chapter we are taught that repentance cannot be national, it too must be individual. Every man must do his own repenting. This is the way the idea finds expression. "Return, O backsliding children, saith the Lord, and I will take you one of a city, and two of a family, and I will bring you to Zion." The repentant sinners shall be received one by one. Possibly there will be only one person out of an entire city, possibly only two persons from a whole clan, but every one who repents will find his way back to Zion. The redeemed will not come in crowds. They will come one by one.

The teaching reaches its climax in the thirty-third and thirty-fourth verses of the thirty-first chapter. "I will put my law in their inward parts, and in their heart will I write it. And they shall teach no more every man his neighbor, and every man his brother, saying, know the Lord, for they shall all know me, from the least of them unto the greatest of them, saith the Lord." This is an amazing declaration. It is an emancipation proclamation for the human mind. The prophet asserts that no man is to be dependent for his knowledge of God on other men, or on groups of men or on institutions. Every man is to do his own thinking, his own repenting. Every man is to form his own convictions. No one else can form them for him. They are to be formed by his own meditations and choices. Every man must cleanse his own heart, enrich his own mind, strengthen his own will. Every man must shoulder his own responsibilities and do his own duty. Religion is not to be a matter of tradition or hearsay, but a matter of personal vision and conviction. Every man is to know God in his own heart. This is the highest peak in the thinking of Jeremiah.

What is the matter with our modern world? Is not one of the secrets of our tribulations the fact that we have lost sight so largely of the individual? He has been slowly disappearing. In some quarters his image has completely faded out. This is due in part to the growth of our cities. The rural population has been for years pouring into our cities, giving us great aggregations of strangers in which the individual is lost in the crowd. We speak familiarly about the "masses," showing by our language that we have lost the outline of the individual man. The man of sixty or seventy who has spent his entire lifetime in a village is an interesting character because of his strong individuality. He thinks for himself, has his own ways of expressing himself. He is original and racy. In the city we are standardized. We think and talk and dress alike. The edges of individuality are blurred. Moreover, we are living in an age of organized activity. We do everything through societies, groups of men organized to accomplish specific ends.

The result is that the business man has disappeared. He has vanished in the corporation. As soon as he enters the room of the Board of Directors we see him no more. He is lost from the public eye. Whatever is done is done by the corporation. And so it has become an adage that a corporation has no soul. Why? Because so many soulless things have been done by corporations within the last fifty years. When wrong things are done, no one man is blamed. It is all the fault of the "system." The individual is excused. The wage-earner has also vanished. He has hidden himself in the Union. He is no

longer accountable for anything he does. It is
the Union which acts. All the diabolical things
which are now done in the realm of industry, are
not done by the individual man. They are done
by the Union. The editor has disappeared. We
once had an editor in New York who was known
by the whole country. His name was Horace
Greeley. We have no editor now—none that we
can see. We have newspaper owners, and they
hire editors, and these editors never sign their
names to anything they write. When you read
an editorial, as you sometimes do, packed full
of sophistry and half truths, you do not know
who wrote it. It is the paper which does the
thinking and the talking. Or to use a term
more dignified and impressive, it is the "Press"
which does the talking and the thinking. Those
big cylinders turned by electricity running the
white paper over the black inked types, it is these
which influence public opinion, and tell us what
we ought to think and do. The politician has also
disappeared. We once had a politician whom
everybody could see. His name was Daniel
Webster, but he vanished long ago. We are now
ruled by political parties. It is the party which
writes the platform. No particular man writes
it. It is the party which conducts the campaign.
Individual men have little to do with it. It is

the party which raises the money, and the party which spends it. Only now and then does the public get interested enough in political matters to tear away all the external coverings and get down to the individual men who are raising and spending the money and making the party what it is.

The Christian is in danger of disappearing. He has a tendency to vanish in the church. In many churches the individual has become invisible. We have been asking, "What is the church doing?" That is a stupid question. You get nowhere by asking a question like that. The important question is: What is Mr. A. doing? He is a prominent man in the church. What is he doing? What is Mr. B. doing? He holds a high position in the church, but what is he doing? What is Mr. C. doing? He has belonged to the church for twenty years. What is he doing? That is the kind of question in which God is interested. That is the question which is all-important and should be answered. It is the conduct of Mr. A. and Mr. B. and Mr. C. which is the key of the church problem. You hear men talking about the amount of money which the church has raised. How much did the church raise last year? It is a bootless question. The question of importance is, How much did Mr. D. give? and how much Mr. E.? and how much Mr. F.? What is the ratio between what these men spend on themselves and what they contribute toward the work of making this a better world? That is the question with which God is concerned, and it is not till that question takes the uppermost place in our own mind that we shall have the key of the problem of church finance.

It is often said that the church of to-day is cold. What makes it cold? The common answer is, "It is the age which makes the church cold. It is a worldly-minded age you know." How shallow! Why make the age a scapegoat? Why not ask, How much ice is there in the heart of Mr. G., and of Mr. H., and of Mr. I.? They are church members, and what is the temperature of their hearts? Is there any fire burning? Is there any spiritual passion in them? It is not the atmosphere of the age which makes the church cold. It is the iciness of the hearts of Mr. G., and Mr. H., and Mr. I. One often hears the lamentation, that the church in our day is impotent. It performs no miracles. It does no mighty works. Why is it impotent? The popular answer is, that the world is not interested in religion. Men are giving their thought to other things. How unsatisfactory! Why not ask a question about Mr. J., and Mr. K., and Mr. L.? They

are church members and the power of the church
depends on them. How much moral energy is
there in Mr. J.? How much spiritual force is
there in Mr. K.? How much strength is there in
Mr. L. when it comes to carrying a cross? We
have a fatal fashion of ignoring the deep questions
and playing with abstractions.

And so the sense of personal responsibility is
growing feeble. Nobody is responsible any more
for anything he does. The criminals are not to
be blamed. Poor men, they are victims and not
culprits. They are not responsible for their
actions. It is society which is to blame. They
are the product of society, and therefore if society
punishes them they are martyrs. They are to be
praised and not condemned.

If we do not blame the murderers and thieves,
we shall not be likely to blame ourselves. A
prominent man said a few years ago that no sensible person worries to-day about his sins. Of
course not. Why should he worry? We are not
responsible for our sins. They are the result of
our heredity. What is heredity? A crowd of
ancestors. A convenient crowd to hide behind.
Our conduct is the result of our environment.
What is environment? A crowd of circumstances
in which we can hide ourselves. By the use of

[85]

big words we slip down into the slough of sloppy thinking.

It is because we lose sight of the individual that we content ourselves with generalizations. We talk about the rich, as though all rich people were alike, and we talk about the poor as though all poor people were alike, and we talk about the youth of to-day as though all young men and all young women were thinking alike and acting alike. There are as many kinds of young people as there are kinds of old people, and it is absurd to sweep them all into one class and speak of them as though they were a unit. Whenever we think of human beings in masses, we think both foolishly and falsely.

We need Jeremiah. Where did he get this idea of the place and power of the individual man? He got it from God. We can be sure of that because Jesus of Nazareth adopted it and made it his own. Did you ever notice that nearly all of the parables of Jesus are organized around a "certain man?" It is a "certain king," a "certain householder," a "certain rich man." He does not tell parables about races or nations or classes. He focuses the eyes on the one man. In the parable of the Prodigal Son, we are not told about fathers or fatherhood, but about one father who had two sons, each son being different from

his brother, and the father dealing with the boys
in two different ways. Every individual stands
out sharp-cut and unforgettable. In that parable
you have the gist of the wisdom which all fathers
and sons need to know. In the parable of the
Good Samaritan, it is "a certain man" who goes
from Jerusalem to Jericho—one man and not a
caravan. It is one priest who passes by, not a
deputation of priests, it is one singer who looks
on, and not the whole choir; it is one Samaritan
who appears and not a committee. Four char-
acters, each one distinct in his own individual
traits; and in that parable you have the essence
of all the wisdom ever needed in the realm of
philanthropy.

Jesus had the individualizing eye. He always
saw the one man. He instinctively picked the
individual out of the crowd. He one day met a
deaf man, and Mark tells us that he took the
man aside from the multitude privately, and dealt
with him there. He was always doing that. He
picked up the blind beggar, and the paralytic at
the pool, and the widow who cast in the two mites,
and the invalid woman who was lost in the crowd.
Peter saw only the crowd; Jesus saw the one
woman who needed him. He picked up his disciples one by one. He did not take his place in
front of the crowd and say, "Come on men, let

us go to work and reform the world." He picked his men. He said: "Come Simon," "Come Andrew," "Come James," "Come John," "Come Nathaniel." Nathaniel was amazed that Jesus knew him. "Where did you see me?" "I saw you under the tree when you were praying, and I made up my mind that you were the kind of man who could help me." I can hear Matthew saying to him, "When did you see me?" I can imagine Jesus replying, "I saw the expression on your face one day when I was preaching in Capernaum, and when I saw the look in your eyes, I said to myself, That man has in him the stuff out of which heroes are made. I will make him one of my helpers." Jesus dealt with each disciple privately. It pierced his heart to be compelled to say, "One of you is going to betray me." He longed for the personal loyalty of each individual heart. When we see him and Peter face to face for the last time, this is the question, "Simon, do you love me?"

Jesus in his mind's eye saw the destruction of Jerusalem and the burning of the Temple, and the blotting out of his nation, but he believed that the world could be saved by one man, one man who belonged wholly to God. It is the message of the Christian religion that the world problem

can be solved by one man. The solution is not
an isolated event but a process, a solution worked
out by one man wholly committed to God, who
is followed by a long succession of men, each one
of them ready to die for the truth.

V

THE INFINITE MAY BE TEMPORARILY THWARTED, BUT CANNOT BE PERMANENTLY DEFEATED

The picture of the potter and the clay is one of the most famous illustrations to be met with in the entire literature of religion. So far as we know, it was original with Jeremiah. If he had never written another paragraph, this one alone would have given him immortal renown. The analogy, once introduced into the mind, began to work with prodigious energy, and one finds the influence of it in many quarters: in the Book of Job, in the Book of Isaiah, in the Book of the Wisdom of Solomon, in the Book of Sirach, in the Letter of Paul to the Romans, in hundreds of volumes written in many lands down to Robert Browning's poem, "Rabbi Ben Ezra." The first half of the eighteenth chapter of the Book of Jeremiah is one of the glorious pages of the Bible. To anyone who is interested in the philosophy of

[90]

religion, it is endlessly fascinating, and enormously suggestive.

Of all the problems with which the human mind has ever grappled, not one is more difficult and formidable than the problem of reconciling the Divine Sovereignty with human free will. The serious mind interested in the deepest things cannot leave that problem alone. It comes back to it again and again. After each long wrestling it becomes weary and seeks relaxation by dealing with simpler questions, but sooner or later it returns again and takes up this ancient puzzle.

There are two assumptions which the normal mind instinctively makes. It assumes that God is sovereign. His word is law. His purpose is unchangeable. He is the absolute ruler of the universe. A God who is not supreme is no God at all. He is victorious. His counsels prevail. His plans are carried out. A defeated God cannot retain the respect of the human intellect. He is not dependent on the caprices and whims of men. He is not at the mercy of feeble, finite creatures like ourselves. A God who can be toyed with by men and outwitted by them is not deserving of the homage of the human heart. We demand a God who is omnipotent. The Divine Sovereignty is a dictum to which we all assent.

The second assumption is that man is free. If

he is not free, our consciousness perpetually deceives us. We all think we are free. We feel free, and our daily experience demonstrates that we are free. We can eat what we please. No matter what the doctor says, we can eat what we choose, and we do it. We can read what we please. No matter what our literary advisers tell us we ought to read, we can read what we will, and we do it. We can come to church or stay at home; we can pray or refuse to pray; we can give our money generously or niggardly. The way is open for us in a thousand directions to do as we please. We can tell a lie or speak the truth. We have done both, and we know how free we are. We can be hateful or loving. We have been both, and we therefore know how easy it is to go either way.

It is not hard to frame an argument against the freedom of the will. Men have been doing that for thousands of years. They are doing it to-day. Many of the arguments are specious and plausible, but they all go to pieces on the rock of experience. No one who has not been befuddled or debauched by the speculations of alleged philosophers ever denies the freedom of the will. The normal man knows and confesses he is free. Samuel Johnson once fell in with a philosopher who started out to prove to him that man is not free, but the sensible old Englishman listened to him with increasing impatience and finally stamping on the floor with his big foot, he thundered, "I know I'm free, and that's the end of it!"

If a man is not free, there is an end of a good many things. If he is not free he is a slave; if a slave, the glory of life has departed. If he is a machine, then there is an end of morality. There is no virtue. There is no vice. A machine cannot be either virtuous or vicious. If he is an automation, a puppet like a figure in a Punch and Judy show, then life is sound and fury, signifying nothing. We know two things. We know that God is supreme, and we know that we are free.

It is at this point that the perennially fascinating unconquerable problem emerges. How can God fore-ordain an event which is contingent on the choice of free creatures? How can God predestine individuals or nations to accomplish specific tasks if men and nations are really free? How can God know that his purposes will ultimately prevail if human beings are free moral agents? How can we be sure that the plans of God will work out successfully if men are actually free? And if we cannot be sure of this, then what becomes of our tranquillity of heart and our joyousness of spirit? These are piercing questions. They cut deep. Men have been debating them

[93]

for centuries, and the debate is not ended. Milton in his "Paradise Lost" tells us of a company of persons who

> Sat on a hill retired,
> In thoughts more elevate, and reasoned high
> Of providence, foreknowledge, will and fate,
> Fixed fate, free-will, foreknowledge absolute;
> And found no end, in wand'ring mazes lost.

One of the reasons why the problem is endlessly fascinating is because one runs a great risk of getting lost.

This, then, is the problem of problems, and I want to look at it with you in the form in which it presented itself to Jeremiah. To understand the Book of Jeremiah and to appreciate the greatness of the prophet, an immense background is necessary. The reason why so many Christians do not understand the book, and therefore do not read it, is because they have not the time for the reading and reflection which are required to put them in possession of the historic background necessary for the understanding of the words which are written.

We must remind ourselves first of all that Jeremiah was a predestinarian as all the other Hebrew prophets were. They believed that God is supreme, that his purposes are eternal and unchangeable, that his designs will be triumphantly carried out. This conviction was rooted deep in the Hebrew heart. The prophets were all certain that it is God who takes the first step. Man does not take it, he cannot take it. God takes the first step everywhere and always. He calls men. Men do not call him. He chooses nations, nations do not choose him. He chose the Hebrew people. The Hebrew race was a chosen race, selected out of many races, to do a specific work for God. It was through this race that all the nations of the earth were to be blessed. Every Hebrew was educated in that joyous belief. The greater the Hebrew and the more spiritual his mind, the more firmly convinced he was that God had chosen his people to manifest his glory to all the world. Every Hebrew prophet looked upon his nation as an individual, peculiarly loved by God and chosen by God to work out one of God's eternal and beneficent designs.

That the Hebrew people was a chosen people was demonstrated, so the prophets thought, by her entire history. God had led the Hebrews out of Egypt, he had given to them the land of Canaan, he had defended them against all their foes, and given them the victory on every great battlefield. He had bestowed upon them prosperity in peace as well as victory in war. That they were in a peculiar sense his own people was certain from unbroken experience extending through many generations.

And so the leaders of the nation came to feel that Israel could not be overthrown. Calamity might overtake other nations but not Israel. Other cities might be destroyed but not Jerusalem. Jerusalem was inviolable, because Jerusalem was the city of the Great King. It was from Jerusalem that the law of God was to go forth to the whole earth. In the eighth century when Sennacherib was thundering across Western Asia, demolishing cities and trampling kingdoms under his feet, Isaiah heartened his countrymen by declaring that Jerusalem could not be captured. The Assyrian monarch would not be permitted to lay a desecrating hand upon the holy city. And it came out just as the prophet had predicted. Sennacherib brought his army to the very gates of Jerusalem, and then all at once something wonderful happened. No one knows just what it was. All we know is that the Assyrian war lord suddenly made up his mind not to attack Jerusalem and took his army home. From that time on, every pious Jew was more firmly convinced than ever that Jerusalem would not and could not be taken by any military power under heaven.

But in the sixth century, only a hundred years

after the preaching of the great Isaiah, a man arose in Jerusalem who told his countrymen that their city was going to fall. He declared that it was going to be completely demolished, that the palaces would be burned, its Temple would go up in smoke, and that even the ark would be lost. This was the most astounding and incredible message which had ever fallen on Jewish ears.

We are not to suppose that Jeremiah arrived at his conclusion in a minute or a day, or even in a week or a month. It may have taken him many years. We are often misled in reading the Bible by the swiftness of its movement and by the compactness of its style. Years are sometimes compressed into a single paragraph. For instance we are told that God said so and so to Jeremiah, and we, lacking imagination, hastily conclude that God spoke to Jeremiah in a moment just as one of us speaks to another. But when God spoke to Jeremiah, he spoke to him through his experience, sometimes through a long protracted experience. He spoke to him through his thinking and his praying and his reflection and his suffering. Little by little a conviction grew up in him, and when that conviction had at last taken complete possession of him, he went before the people saying, "Thus saith the Lord."

It is not likely that Jeremiah saw the destination of the city and the nation when he first began to preach. He knew that things were in a bad way, but he was not hopeless. He hoped that the nation could be reformed. He did his best to save it. He began his work by denouncing the city. He uncovered its ulcers and its running sores. He hurled thunderbolts at its prophets and priests and princes. He poured the vials of his wrath upon its corruptions. But all this came to nothing. He could not induce repentance by denunciation. And so he tried warnings. He uttered threats. He painted lurid pictures of the frightful doom which was surely coming. But this also availed nothing. The people could not be scared out of their sins. And so he resorted to argument. He appealed to their reason. He tried to convince them that they were stupid, and that their course was contrary to reason. But they could not be argued out of their senseless and dangerous ways. Finally he appealed to the angels of their better nature. He pleaded with them. He exhorted them by the mercies of God to do better. But they turned a deaf ear to his entreaties and he finally gave up all hope. He became convinced that the nation had sinned beyond all possibility of repentance, and that there was nothing to do but to inform the people of the awful doom which was certain to overtake them. The Ethiopian cannot change his skin, the leopard cannot change his spots, Israel cannot change its way! He came at last to feel that even prayer for Israel was futile. There comes a time when even God does not want to be entreated. The time for prayer is gone. Sin, after it has reached a certain stage, cannot be removed by praying. One day the prophet told the people that even if Moses, the greatest of their lawgivers, and Samuel, the greatest of their judges, should unitedly plead with God for the people, their prayers would come to nothing, and God would say to them, "Get this people out of my sight!"

Right here there emerged a problem, a vexing, unescapable, baffling problem, a problem for the intellect, and also for the heart, a problem which gave the prophet no rest day or night. Here is the question. If Jerusalem is going to fall and the Israelitish nation is going to be blotted out, what becomes of the Word of God? God was supposed to have a purpose. What has become of his purpose? Is his purpose to be defeated? Will it be defeated? What becomes of the plan of God? Is his plan to be frustrated? Is the rebelliousness of Israel to overcome the will of God? What becomes of the promises of God? Are they to be broken? What becomes of the oath of God? He swore to the fathers of

[99]

Israel that he would never forsake them, that he would be their God forever. What becomes of all the teachings of the poets and all the predictions of the prophets and all the instructions of the wise men of Israel, if Jerusalem is to be demolished and the Temple consumed and the ark destroyed and the people, God's people, are to be scattered abroad? If Jerusalem is indeed to fall and Judah to be beaten down into a heap of dust, "The pillared firmament is rottenness and earth's base built on stubble." That was the agony in the prophet's heart. You read his pages and almost go to sleep, because it all seems so tame and dull; but if you only had the information and the imagination, you would hear the hissing of the red-hot lava which runs in boiling streams below the surface of the tranquil language of this ancient book.

For a long time the prophet worked in perplexity and despondency. He could not think his problem through. He floundered in darkness. He talked with God, argued with him, remonstrated with him, quarreled with him, but no light came. But one day a ray of light suddenly broke upon him. He caught a glimpse of a great truth which he had never grasped before, a truth which gave him encouragement and peace. The light came to him in a pottery in the south end of

Jerusalem. That day became a red letter day in his memory. He felt sure that God had put the impulse into his heart to go into that pottery on that particular day, and he had no doubt that it was God who had spoken to him there. He did what we sometimes do. If now and then we do something or say something which leads to blessed results, we say, "I do not know how I came to do it. It must have been God who guided me!"

This visit to the pottery is one of the most interesting episodes in the whole Bible. Some of its importance comes from the fact that it throws light on the nature of inspiration and gives us an inkling of the way in which prophets were led into the apprehension of new ideas. We are in the habit of saying that the prophets were inspired, but we do not know what that means. Inspiration is to us a sort of magic and nobody can understand it. We say that the prophets had truth revealed to them, and that too remains a deep mystery. We do not deny inspiration for that would result in our being classed with the infidels, and we accept the idea that holy men of old spake as they were moved by the Holy Spirit, but it is all so far removed from anything which happens now that it makes the Bible seem foreign and religion an impenetrable mystery. It is not often the Bible takes us into its confidence and lets us see how the revelation came. Here is an instance in which we are told the exact circumstances amidst which a new idea was born in a prophet's brain. Strange to say the idea did not come to him in the Temple, but in a workshop. He did not get his flash of insight while he was praying, but while he was watching a potter engaged in his daily work. God reveals himself in strange places and at unexpected seasons. For instance he once revealed himself in a stable. In a different way he revealed a great truth one day in a pottery.

A potter's shop in the sixth century before Christ was a dull and commonplace room. Machinery in those days was primitive and crude. Men worked with few and simple tools. The machine of the potter consisted of two discs, a big one and a little one, made sometimes of stone and sometimes of wood, the little one placed on the top of the big one, the big one stationary and the little one revolving horizontally on that. The upper disc was turned by a treadle worked by one foot of the potter. The interesting feature in the room, however, was not the machine but the workman.

We can imagine the pleasure which came to Jeremiah as he watched this potter at his work. It is always interesting to see some one do something. Let a man do a thing as simple as digging a hole in a street, and a group of men will gather around him to watch him do it. Let a man or a woman do something in a shop window, and there will be a crowd in front of the window all day long. Let a man in a restaurant bake buckwheat cakes in a window, and he will never lack an interested audience. It is almost as interesting to see a cake baked as to eat it. The interest increases in proportion to the skill displayed in performing the achievement. To mold clay into vessels of beauty requires skill. If you have never seen a potter at work you have missed something. The thing which surprises one most is the swiftness and ease with which the potter performs his miracles. All he does, apparently, is to put his hands on the clay, and in a few moments the clay becomes the thing he wants it to be. You feel you could do it yourself. Jeremiah watched the potter with delight.

He got not only pleasure but an idea. The reason he got an idea was because he had been doing a lot of hard thinking. We always see the world through our mind. What you see in the world depends largely on what you carry in your head. A man in love sees the world through his love. This explains why the world to him is so radiant. Love is the most beautiful thing in the world, and the world looked at through love sparkles. But let a man look at the world through a grief, and the world is gray. He may try to convince himself that the world is not gray, but it is gray because he sees it through his sorrow. Or let a man look at the world through a wrong, a wrong done to him or his parents, and the world to him becomes hideous. One must remember this in trying to understand the conduct of certain groups of radicals. It is because they look at our civilization through a wrong that has been done them that they want to tear our social order to pieces. It is ugly in their eyes and they hate it.

Men often see the world through the dominant problem which they carry in their mind. When Archimedes saw the water pouring over the rim of his bathtub, he got an idea, because he had been mulling a problem in physics for many a day. Galileo got an idea from the swinging of the chandelier in the cathedral at Pisa, because he saw it through a mind which had been vexed by a problem. Sir Isaac Newton got an idea from a falling apple, because he saw it through the problem which he had been working at for months. The apple spoke to him because he had been puzzled by the moon and the stars. If you want the universe to speak to you, you must have questions in your mind. If you want God to reveal anything to you, you must do a deal of serious thinking. Jeremiah had been thinking for years on a problem which teased and tormented him, and his mind had become so sensitized that it was ready to snatch up new impressions. It was susceptible to new ideas. In the process of revelation God and man work together.

The phenomenon which especially attracted the prophet's attention on that day, was the way in which the potter was thwarted in his work. Sometimes the clay would not become what he wanted it to be. It seemed to be stubborn and refused to bend to the potter's will. It was stiff and obstinate, it had a lump in it or some foreign substance like a pebble had become imbedded in it, and the progress of the potter was checked. But what struck Jeremiah was the fact that the potter was never disgusted by the refractory attitude of the clay. He did not destroy it, nor did he throw it away. He went right on with his work. He simply crushed the clay into a shapeless mass and proceeded to make something else. He was not at all discouraged. He did not lock up the shop and go home. He kept on working. If he could not make the vessel he started out to make, he made another one, equally serviceable and equally beautiful. At the end of the day his work was satisfactory and complete.

He had been thwarted, but he was not defeated.

In that hour a new idea flashed upon the prophet. As he expressed it, "God spoke to him!" The idea flashed on him that God was the Potter, the Supreme Potter of the universe, and that Israel was a lump of clay which God was molding into a vessel for his use. But Israel was stubborn, rebellious, perverse, refusing to do what it ought to do, and so God was going to crush it by suffering and exile. But he would not throw the clay away. The city would be destroyed, but another would rise from the ashes. There would be a new Jerusalem. The Temple would be burned, but there would be a second temple, a new temple. The old covenant written on tables of stone would be annulled, but there would be a new covenant written on the heart. A fresh revelation had been given to the human mind through Jeremiah, and the prophet that day went back to his home tranquilized and strengthened.

In that conception of the Divine Potter and the human clay you have one of the great achievements of the human intellect. It was twenty-five hundred years ago that Jeremiah caught his vision of the Almighty as the potter and humanity as the clay, and down to the present hour that remains the best figure in our possession for the reconciliation of predestination and freedom. It is a

remarkable fact that in the long sweep of twenty-
five hundred years, not a man out of the long
procession of clever and gifted and brilliant
writers and thinkers has been able to conceive an
illustration so good as the one which Jeremiah
found in the little pottery in South Jerusalem.
It will probably remain forever the most satisfying image which man can form of the Divine
Sovereignty in relation to the freedom of the will.

The figure grows more impressive and more
beautiful the better we understand the structure
and ongoing of the world. We know from our
study of history that God does crush nations.
Many empires and republics have been squeezed
into a shapeless mass by his almighty hands. But
he does not blot out the human race. It lives on.
He does not destroy the world. He could do it.
He could drown it or burn it up, or blow it to
atoms, but he does not do it. He keeps on working. He does not become discouraged. He does
not shut up this little shop. What is the earth
but a tiny pottery rolling round the sun? The
potter is still working in his shop. His hands
are still on the clay. If they were not, the future
would be hopeless.

He has not surrendered his ideal. He will
never give up his plan. His eternal purpose will
be carried out. It is his will that all men shall

be conformed to the image of his son. He has decided to judge the world by one man whom he has ordained. It is his purpose that all men and nations shall stand before the judgment seat of Christ. He will never coerce a nation to pursue a course it does not choose to follow, but he will crush that nation if it is rebellious, by calamity and suffering into a shapeless mass, and then proceed to work upon it afresh. Never will the human will be ignored or trampled on, but mankind, if perverse and foolish, must suffer again and again for all its disobedience. The patience of the Infinite Potter is inexhaustible, and he will go on with his work till the human heart of its own accord surrenders, till every knee bows to Christ and every tongue confesses that he is Lord indeed. "Our wills are ours we know not how. Our wills are ours to make them thine."

The whole message of religion concerning the Divine Sovereignty and human freedom is beautifully expressed in a little Hebrew poem which we call the Second Psalm:

Why do the nations rage,
And the peoples meditate a vain thing?
The kings of the earth set themselves,
And the rulers take counsel together,
Against the Lord, and against his anointed, saying,
Let us break their bonds asunder,

And cast away their cords from us!
He that sitteth in the heavens laughs—
The Lord holds them in derision.
He has set up his Son as King upon the holy hill
      of Zion.
His Son has been made the Master of the earth.
He will break nations with a rod of iron.
He will dash them in pieces like a potter's
      vessel.
Now, therefore, be wise, O kings,
Be instructed ye judges of the earth,
Serve the Lord with reverence,
And rejoice with awe,
Render homage to the Son,
Lest you end in ruin.
Blessed are all who take refuge in him.

VI

THE LAW IN THE HEART IS THE SOLE
BASIS OF PERMANENT
REFORMATION

The Book of Jeremiah reaches its highest peak
in the thirty-first chapter. The culminating words
are: "I will make a new covenant with the house
of Israel, and with the house of Judah, says
Jehovah. I will put my law in their inward parts
and in their heart will I write it." Heaven and
earth shall pass away, but these words shall not
pass away, because the Son of God has made them
his own. On the last night of his earthly life, our
Lord met with his intimate friends in the City of
Jerusalem, and while they sat around the dinner
table, he passed a cup of wine from one man to another, saying, "This is the cup of the New Covenant in my blood." At a grave moment in his
life and at a crisis in the history of the world, our
Lord showed that he was thinking of Jeremiah.
He had an idea of Jeremiah in his mind, and
quoted an expression that Jeremiah had used six

hundred years before. The conception of the New Covenant was Jeremiah's greatest idea. The sentence spoken by Jesus made a deep impression on all who heard it, and also on all to whom that sentence was repeated. Matthew wrote it down in his Gospel. So did Mark, so did Luke; and Paul in his First Letter to the Corinthians quotes the sentence as one of the treasures he had received from Peter, James and John. In his Second Letter to the Corinthians, Paul shows he is still thinking of Jeremiah. The idea of the New Covenant is yet in his mind. "Ye are our epistle written in our hearts. Ye are an epistle of Christ ministered by us, written not with ink, but with the Spirit of the living God; not in tables of stone, but in tables that are hearts of flesh. God has made us ministers of a new covenant; not of the letter but of the Spirit; for the letter killeth, but the Spirit giveth life."

The writer of the Letter to the Hebrews is also full of the idea of the New Covenant. The word "covenant" occurs seventeen times in his letter, and the ninth chapter of the letter is devoted entirely to contrasting the New Covenant with the Old. The writer of the letter gives Jesus a new title, one not given to him elsewhere, "The Mediator of a New Covenant."

It is not surprising, therefore, that when the

writings of the Evangelists and Apostles were
finally gathered together into a single volume,
some one called the book the "New Covenant."
It was because of what Matthew and Mark and
Luke had recorded, and what Paul and the writer
of the Letter to the Hebrews had said that the
early Christians came to call the Christian Bible
the "New Covenant."

If some one at this point should ask why if the
early Christians called our Christian Bible the
"New Covenant," we call it the "New Testament," the answer is this: Any one who glances
even hurriedly through the books of the Old
Testament, cannot fail to notice the frequent
occurrence of the word "Covenant." It occurs as
many as one hundred and ten times in five Old
Testament Books. We read of the "Book of the
Covenant," and of the "blood of the Covenant,"
and of the "tables of the Covenant," and of the
"ark of the Covenant." The Hebrew preachers
loved to preach about the Covenant, and the
Hebrew poets were fond of singing about it. The
word "Covenant" was often on the lips of the
religious leaders because the Covenant idea was
deep in the Jewish mind and heart. A Covenant,
as you know, is an agreement or arrangement, a
compact or contract, a mutual promise between
two parties. One party agrees to do a certain

thing, and in return the other party promises to do something else. The Hebrews always thought of religion as being based on a Covenant. God made a Covenant with Abraham and renewed it with Isaac, and again renewed it with Jacob, and finally through Moses made it with the entire people of Israel. God said to Israel, "I will be your God," and Israel said to God, "I will be your people." God said to Israel, "If you obey me, I will protect you and bless you," and the people said to God, "If you will be our God we will obey you and keep your law." It was because of their confidence in the reality of this Covenant between Jehovah and his people, that the faith of the prophets was unwavering, and the hearts of the statesmen were undaunted.

The first Christians were Hebrews, and they naturally thought and spoke after the manner of Hebrews. The idea of a Covenant was deep-rooted in their minds. When they talked about their religious experience, the word "Covenant" came spontaneously to their lips. The first Christian writers wrote in Greek, and it was necessary for them to find a Greek word which would accurately translate the Hebrew word meaning "Covenant." They found a word, but unfortunately it was somewhat ambiguous, for sometimes it meant "covenant" and other times it meant a "will." A covenant is an agreement whereas a will is a legal document disposing of a man's property after his death. A will has no force till after the death of the person who has made it. This ambiguous Greek word was used thirty-three times by the men who wrote our New Testament.

Near the end of the fourth century, a man by the name of Jerome translated the Greek Testament into Latin. When he found the Greek word meaning "Covenant" he translated it by the Latin word, "Testamentum," a technical legal word meaning will. In the fourteenth century when John Wycliffe translated the Latin Testament into English, he followed Jerome's example and used the word "testament," simply cutting off the last two letters of "testamentum" to make the word English. When William Tyndale translated the New Testament in the sixteenth century, he was largely influenced by Wycliffe, and so he also used the word "testament." In the seventeenth century when a group of British scholars under the patronage of King James I made a new translation of the New Testament, they saw that the use of the word "testament" was in many instances incorrect, and so in twenty places they employed the word "covenant," and only in thirteen cases did they use the word "testament." When near the end of the nineteenth century, a group of

English scholars and a group of American scholars combined to make a new translation of the New Testament, they used "covenant" thirty-one times, and "testament" only twice. They used "testament" twice because the writer of the Letter to the Hebrews in the ninth chapter of that letter uses the Greek word expressly and incontestably in the sense of "will," thus leaving the translators no option. But in every other place the Greek word is given its customary meaning, "covenant." In the King James Version we have always read, "This cup is the New Testament in my blood." But in the Revised Version we read, "This cup is the New Covenant in my blood." In the King James Version we have read, "God has made us ministers of the New Testament," but in the Revised Version the sentence runs, "God has made us ministers of the New Covenant." In the King James Version we have read, "He is the Mediator of the New Testament," but the Revisers have changed that to "He is the Mediator of a New Covenant." One would suppose after these changes that the Revisers would change the title of the "New Testament," and call it the "New Covenant," but this they did not venture to do. They felt this would be going too far. There is always a popular prejudice against a new version of a holy book, and the Revisers did not want to queer their translation by doing anything so radical as to change the title by which the English Bible had for centuries been known. And so on the title page of the new translation they wrote the words, "The New Testament of our Lord and Savior Jesus Christ." This is what the English Revisers did, but the American Revisers were bolder. They wrote on the title page of their translation, "The New Covenant, commonly known as the New Testament of our Lord and Savior Jesus Christ." This is as far as they dared go, and it was far enough. They gave us the correct title and then confessed that everybody calls it the "New Testament." That is what the English-speaking people are likely to call it to the end of time. The title "New Testament" is too sacred to the heart ever to be superseded. But it is a pity that the true title has been lost. We lose something by calling our Christian Bible the "New Testament." A testament is from the dead whereas a covenant is between the living, and the idea which we ought to strive to keep alive in our mind is that our Bible is the account of a new covenant between the living soul and the living God. In the celebration of the Lord's Supper, we should remember that Christ said, "This is the cup of the new covenant" instead of "This is the cup of the New Testament," for at the Lord's table we are helped by remembering that this sacrament commemorates the new compact made between God and the soul, and established by the blood of his Son.

While we say with our lips, "The New Testament," let us say in our heart, "The New Covenant." Let us never forget that it was Jeremiah who coined the title of our sacred book. Let us never cease to regret that it was owing to a slip in getting his idea over from one language to another that our Bible has a title which none of its authors ever intended it should have, a title which obscures to all but a few our indebtedness to the great prophet of Anathoth.

How did the prophet get the idea of a new covenant? He got it when the old covenant broke down. The old covenant broke down in this way. The Hebrews lived under a monarchy. Some of these kings were good and others were bad. In the eighth century they had a good king, Hezekiah, a man who feared God and endeavored to do his will. In the seventh century they had a bad king, Manasseh, a man who was not only nonreligious but even anti-religious. At least he cared nothing for the religion of Jehovah. He was the son of Hezekiah. It is a singular fact that a good man can have a bad son. Manasseh had the notion that all religions are alike. One is no better than the other because they all aim at the same thing. During his reign the religious cults of surrounding nations penetrated Judah. The Egyptian religion got a hold on the Jewish imagination. The king even named one of his sons "Amon" after one of the Egyptian gods, an amazing thing for a Jewish King to do. The Assyrian religion came in and Jews began to worship the moon and stars. Altars were built in many a housetop and sacrifices were offered to the heavenly bodies. Astarte, the goddess of sensual love was imported from Phœnicia, became a great favorite among the people, and a statue of her was set up even in the Temple in Jerusalem. Along with these religions came idols. In every part of the land could be seen the images of pagan gods. Polytheism was once more enthroned. The old superstitions of the Canaanitish cults came in again, and with these came many an abomination.

As the religious life sank lower the number of charletans increased, astrologers and fortune tellers and clairvoyants and wizards and witches and healers of various sorts, imposters who in a time of religious declension fatten on the credulity of the ignorant. Sensuality flowed in like a flood, as it always does when religion goes down. Religion is the only power that can keep sensuality in check. Philosophy cannot do it nor can science nor can

law nor can ethical instruction. Nothing can overcome sensuality but religion, and only religion of
the highest type. Along with the demoralization
of religious faith, came a wild fanaticism. A cruel
bigotry swept over the land. The devotees of
low ideals always hate and scorn the defenders of
high ideals. The prophets of Jehovah were hated
and hounded. Some of them were imprisoned
and others were killed. Most of them were
driven into hiding. The moral degradation of the
nation was complete. In a monarchy, fashionable
society always follows the king. Judah followed
Manasseh in his idolatries and infidelities, and
some families sank so low that they even sacrificed
their children to Moloch.

But kings like other men must die, and after a
reign of forty-five years, Manasseh slept with his
fathers. His son Amon succeeded him, but was
assassinated within two years. Amon's son,
Josiah, a boy of eight, was now made king. The
government rested for several years in the hands
of a group of royal counselors, who were both
able and pious. The horrors of the preceding
reign had united them and had kindled in them a
fire of new devotion to Jehovah.

When the king was eighteen years old, a book
was found one day in one of the rooms of the
Temple, an ancient law book which was said to

have been written by Moses. So far as the scholars are able to discover, this book was in substance
our Book of Deuteronomy. In this book the covenant between Jehovah and his people is magnified.
Blessings are promised to the obedient, and curses
are pronounced on those who disobey. The book
was read to the king, who was deeply stirred and
alarmed by what he heard. If the book contained
indeed the Word of God, then the nation had gone
far astray and only swift repentance could save
it from ruin. A national convention was called in
Jerusalem and a great reform movement was in-
augurated. It was decided to extirpate idolatry
root and branch. To accomplish this it was de-
creed that all the local sanctuaries throughout the
land should be abolished. The offering of sacrifices was permitted only in the Temple in Jerusalem. As there was only one God, there should
be only one National Temple.

The program was a radical one, and the condi-
tions for carrying it out were ideal. The reform
had behind it the power of the king. He was
young and full of zeal. He had none of the timid-
ities and scruples which often come with advancing years. He was not afarid of going too far.
He was determined at all risks to make the work
of cleansing complete. He was backed up by a
group of men who were eager to carry out the

king's plans. There is much to be said in favor of monarchy, and especially in favor of absolute monarchy. When all political power is lodged in the hands of one man, if that man is both strong and good, something is sure to get done. Things are done swiftly and with efficiency. Laws can be passed without delay, and these laws can be enforced without successful opposition. Officials lose their heads if they do not do their work well. The most damning indictment of popular government is its lack of efficiency and its exasperating delays. It takes forever to get anything worth while accomplished, and when it is done it is often done in an extravagant and bungling manner. In a democracy it is Tom, Dick and Harry who get into office, and when once there they have a fatal propensity to talk.

Modern parliamentary government has gone on the rocks in more than one country because of the loquacity of the representatives of the people. In Turkey, Kemal Pasha has accomplished more in the way of reform in ten years than the Turkish Parliament could have accomplished in a hundred years. The Turkish politicians are notoriously vocal, and they will talk on for years, accomplishing nothing. In Italy things went on from bad to worse until finally Mussolini disgusted with it all came boldly to the front saying, "I will take

Has he now?!!

these matters into my own hands and attend to them myself." In five years he has rooted out more abuses and introduced more reforms than could have been accomplished in fifty years by the Parliament of Italy. It was the perpetual gabble of the House of Commons in England which drove Carlyle into his idolization of Frederick the Great and Oliver Cromwell. He was so sick of what he called the "babblement and twaddlement" of the alleged rulers of England, that he spent his life in singing the praises of silence. It is the tragedy of America, that in the City Hall and in the State House and in the National Capitol, there is so much chatter and so little accomplished. Important laws are passed only after disgusting delays, and when they are passed they are enforced only feebly or not at all.

It was not so in ancient Palestine in the days of good King Josiah. The king and his counselors decided that the nation should be reformed, and it was. No such reformation had ever been known in Israel before. The work of destruction was carried on with ruthless hands. The asheras, or wooden posts, by the side of every Canaanitish shrine, were cut down. The altars were demolished. The high places were polluted. The wooden idols were burnt, the stone idols were ground to powder, the metal idols were beaten out of shape. The lazy and ignorant priests were driven out of business. The whole land was swept clean as with a new broom. In Jerusalem everything was changed. The temple was cleansed of the idolatrous emblems. The statue of Astarte was removed. The worship of Jehovah was made more elaborate and gorgeous. The number of sacrifices was enormously increased. The stream of flowing blood was continuous and full. There were more songs and more prayers, more burnt offerings and more festivals. The crowds in the temple courts were unprecedentedly large, and Jehovah was worshiped with a zeal and a pomp which had been unknown for many generations. The reformation was a glorious success!

And then one day something terrible happened. Josiah died. He was killed in battle. He was young, only thirty-nine. The reformation had gone forward only thirteen years when the heavens were darkened and the nation was plunged into unconsolable grief by the death of the young ruler. He was succeeded by a weakling, and the weakling was followed by a crafty politician who was stupid, and his successor was another political nobody. Little by little the results of the reformation were wiped out. The old abuses crept in again. The old diseases broke out afresh. The old corruptions stole back again. The people fell back into their old habits, and the nation slid down into the old rut.

In Jerusalem there was a man, the Prophet Jeremiah, who looked with sad eyes on all this, and who meditated on it in his heart. He saw that changing the place of worship is not enough, and that changing the forms of worship is not enough. He saw that changing the system is not sufficient, and that altering the machinery is not sufficient. He saw that you cannot reform an institution by making changes on the surface, and that you cannot reform a nation by a law written on two slabs of stone, or by a law written in a book. If a nation is to be truly reformed, the law must be written in its heart. The law in the heart is the sole basis of a lasting reform. He saw that the old covenant was of no avail. The tables of the covenant were to be destroyed. The ark of the covenant was to be lost. The covenant itself was to be abrogated. God would not keep his promise because the people had not kept theirs. He would not keep it because he could not keep it. All his promises are conditional. He cannot protect a people which does not obey him. He cannot bless a nation which tramples on his law. Israel was disobedient. The City was therefore doomed, the temple was doomed, the ark was

[124]

doomed, the nation was doomed. The covenant was a thing of the past.

It is at this point that the greatness of Jeremiah comes into view. A small man can see when it is growing dark. A small man is able to see destruction when it is at the door. He can paint lurid pictures of approaching doom, but he cannot see beyond the darkness. He does not know how to put a sunbeam into his picture. A great man pierces the darkness and sees the glory of a hidden dawn. A small man can see that the patient is very sick. He can describe the symptoms and make a thorough diagnosis, but he cannot suggest a remedy. A great man knows not only the disease, but he also knows the cure. The small man always indulges in foolish hopes. He deceives himself and also others. He thinks the patient will get well, because he hopes he will get well. The great man knows when the patient is sick unto death, and says so. He will not fool himself nor will he mislead others. Jeremiah was a great physician. He saw that Israel was sick unto death. He said so. He saw that the nation was going to die. But this did not daunt him. The old covenant was abrogated. But this was not the end of God's resources. God could make another covenant, a different kind of covenant. God could write a covenant on the heart. God would now write, not with his finger, but with his spirit, not on tables of stone but on the tables of the heart. This is what God would some day do. He would break the nation to pieces, but on the individual heart he would write his law. He would make a new covenant with the House of Israel and with the House of Judah. He would put his law into their inward parts and in their hearts he would write it. He would be their God, and they would be his people. He would forgive their iniquity, and their sin he would remember no more.

Do you observe how high we have come? We are almost up to the level of the New Testament. We are in the vicinity of Jesus. We can overhear Jesus saying, "You must be borne again." That is an idea of Jeremiah expressed in Jesus' way. We can overhear Jesus saying, "God is spirit, and they who worship him, must worship him in spirit and in truth." That is an idea of Jeremiah stated in a phraseology slightly altered. But there are some things we cannot hear from the mountain top in Jeremiah. We cannot hear Jesus say, "This is the cup of the new covenant in my blood." Jeremiah never foresaw the Mediator of the New Covenant. He saw the New Covenant, but he did not see the Mediator of it. He saw the ideal which was to be worked out in the heart, but he did not know by what means that ideal was to be realized. He did not see Jesus. Nor can we in Jeremiah hear Jesus saying, "In my Father's house are many mansions. If it were not so I would have told you. I go to prepare a place for you. And if I go, I will come again and receive you unto myself." From the Book of Jeremiah we cannot hear that. The preacher cannot find in Jeremiah a text for Easter Sunday. There is no Easter in the calendar of Jeremiah. The idea of immortality never came into any of his sermons, nor so far as we can tell, did that idea ever enter his mind. God spoke to the fathers in the prophets by divers portions and in divers manners, and he has spoken unto us in his Son. Jeremiah saw in part and prophesied in part, but when he who is perfect came, then all that Jeremiah had said was swallowed up in the glory of the final truth. We can go a long way up the mountain side with Jeremiah, but when we reach the highest slopes, we discover that the prophet is no longer by our side. On lifting up our eyes we see no man but Jesus only.

VII

A SICK HEART IS THE SOURCE OF THE WORLD'S WOE

One of the key sentences of the Book of Jeremiah is found in the seventeenth chapter, verse 9: "The heart is deceitful above all things and desperately wicked." That is the way the sentence stands in our King James Version, but in the English Revised Version the sentence reads: "The heart is deceitful above all things and it is desperately sick." Dr. George Adam Smith, probably the ablest living interpreter of the Hebrew prophets, also prefers the word "sick." He translates the sentence thus: "False above all is the heart, and sick to despair." You will notice that he drops the word "desperately" and substitutes "to despair." The scholars have had difficulty in agreeing on the best word by which to translate the Hebrew adverb before the adjective "sick." Our American Revisers preferred the word "exceedingly," some scholars prefer the word "incurably," and these latter are strengthened in

Ch 17:9

their choice by the fact that in two other places in this book the same adverb is translated "incurably." Still other scholars prefer the adverb "mortally." They all agree that the adverb is a strong one. The sickness is most serious. We express the idea of the Hebrew word when we say "fearfully sick" or "terribly sick." Some of us would probably say "awfully sick." It was the prophet's deep conviction that the human heart is sick, not slightly or temporarily sick, but dangerously and alarmingly sick.

What is the matter with this world? All thoughtful men agree that there is something the matter with it, something radically and tremendously wrong, and its condition does not seem to greatly improve. What is the root of our trouble? In what quarter shall we look for the fountainhead of our misery? What is the bottom cause of our woe?

An early answer to the question was that the root of our trouble lies in the physical creation. Matter is an enemy of God. Matter is the seat of evil. Spirit and matter are opposed to each other. A man's body is the cause of his undoing. His body is vile. His flesh is the seat of his appetites and passions, and it is these which tear human life to pieces. This is the answer which the East has given from the beginning.

Wherever this philosophy prevails, the ascetic view of life becomes dominant. If the human body is the source of the world's tragedy, then the body must be beaten down into submission. The flesh must be humiliated, cudgeled, starved, despised. Desire must be dampened and if possible extinguished. All the natural inclinations and cravings of human nature must be crucified. In the temples and along the roads of India one sees multitudes of so-called "holy men," who look like skeletons. They have waged a long warfare against the body.

This Asiatic idea of life leaked into Europe, and by and by trickled into the Christian Church, and flowered out in medieval monasticism. It was never a native part of the Christian religion, but a foreign importation. For a thousand years it poisoned and impoverished the Christian Church. Multitudes of the best men in Europe felt it to be their duty to get away from the world of things. Social life and business life and even family life were counted corrupting and unclean. Men underwent long fasts, and beat their backs, and slept on stones, in an effort to break the power of the body which they felt was an enemy of God. It was a devastating delusion, and the human race could not be forever holden of it. Little by little its power was broken, and now in the West it lurks only in isolated and darkened corners. Our Western common sense has thrown it off as a silly superstition and a deadly error.

In the year 1712 there was born in the city of Geneva a man whose name is familiar to us all, Jean Jacques Rousseau. He was a romancer, a dreamer, a rebel against society. He believed that man is naturally good, but that men everywhere are bad. They are bad because they have been corrupted by civilization. They have been degraded by progress, deceived by their knowledge, perverted by their institutions, and enslaved by their inherited customs and conventions. At the beginning men were happy and free, now they are everywhere in chains. The only hope for mankind is in a return to the state of nature. Men must get away from this social state which is incurably bad. Children must be educated in isolation from society in order that their natural qualities may develop. His book entitled *Contrat Social* is one of the most influential books ever written. More than any other one volume it brought on the French Revolution. Rousseau has been dead one hundred and fifty years, and his influence is mighty still. His ideas have taken many forms and given rise to many Utopian dreams. They have formed the basis of many a socialistic scheme. Ever since his day, it has been the fashion to make society the scapegoat for all our troubles. We call it now the "social order." We are handicapped and cursed, reformers are always telling us, by our "social system."

Our civilization is a stumbling block and a curse. The human race is sick. Humanity is an invalid. Mankind has been placed on the operating table and the doctors have gathered round the table to make an examination of the patient. We have never had so many social doctors as we have to-day. And they have never been so well equipped as now. They have instruments to see with and to hear with and to probe with and to cut with. We have never had so many nurses waiting with chart and pencil to jot down the changing symptoms, and to chronicle every variation in temperature and respiration and pulse beat.

Every physician makes his own diagnosis, and the conflicting reports which they give us form an interesting and bewildering story. One physician tells us that our trouble is Capitalism. Capitalism is the serpent which has crawled into our Eden. The world was happy before Capitalism got its grip upon us, and there will be no happiness again until this snake has been crushed. Many persons believe that. Another physician tells us that our chief trouble is Commercialism. The whole world has been commercialized, and that is the cause of our degradation. We can never bring back the true tone to life until we cast out this commercialistic devil. Many persons are sure of that. Still another specialist asserts that our worst malady is Sectionalism. One section of the population is arrayed against another section, one class of society is clamoring for special privileges at the expense of another class. This is the most virulent disease by which our Western World is just now afflicted. There are many persons who are convinced of that. Some experts say that the deadliest curse of the modern world is Nationalism, a bloated arrogant exaltation of national honor and prestige. They claim that it was Nationalism which precipitated the World War, and that unless we curb or destroy this nationalistic spirit, the disasters ahead of us will surpass those of the past. Not a few subscribe to this. There are other doctors, only a few, however, in number, who think that our deadliest enemy is Internationalism. This is a subtle poison which is being injected secretly into the veins of the body politic, and unless we are on our guard, the entire social fabric is going to dissolve. All the doctors agree that the patient is horribly sick, but they cannot agree in regard to the nature of the malady. Dean Inge, the Christian, and Bertrand

Russell, the atheist, are equally certain that society is desperately sick.

Because the diagnoses do not agree, we have a wide variety of suggested remedies. Some doctors think that Socialism is the only possible cure. Others say that Socialism is not radical enough. Nothing short of Communism will meet the needs of the situation. In Italy there are many who feel that Fascism is the only remedy which will prove efficacious. While in Russia a multitude of social doctors think that Sovietism is the only nostrum which will heal the open sore of the world. In every country there are groups of men who feel certain that Anarchism holds in its hand the key which will open the gate through which humanity will sweep into the golden age.

The doctors do not agree either as to the disease, or as to its cure. They agree in this one thing only—the world is desperately sick. The spirit of our age, in the words of Matthew Arnold, has taken

> the suffering human race
> And read each wound, each weakness clear,
> And struck its finger on the place,
> And said, "Thou ailest here and here."

The pity is that the fingers of the doctors have fallen on so many different spots, we do not know just where the root of our trouble lies.

Turning away for a moment from the confusion of our generation, let us sit for a little while at the feet of an ancient thinker, one of the greatest thinkers of all time, the Hebrew Prophet Jeremiah. Some of you never think of him as a great thinker. You do not class him with great thinkers, because you do not go back far enough. You go back to Plato, but this man Jeremiah died a hundred and fifty years before Plato was born. You never go back that far. You do not think it worth while. You go back perhaps even to Pericles, but this man Jeremiah died nearly one hundred years before Pericles was born. You assume that the first deep thinking ever done upon our planet, was done in Greece, but you are mistaken in that assumption. The first deep thinking in regard to God and man done in this world, was not done in Greece or Rome, not in Egypt or Assyria, not in India or in China, but in Palestine. The deepest thinkers which the ancient world produced were the Hebrew prophets, and of these none is deeper than Jeremiah. What does this man say in regard to the malady of the world? He lived in the sixth century before Christ and faced the same problem which we are facing now. The world is desperately sick to-day, and it was desperately sick then. Jeremiah was a keen observer. He had wonderful eyes. Nothing escaped those eyes of his. His eyes saw to the roots of things. He noted the symptoms. He studied the patient. Year after year he patiently watched and brooded. After many years of observation and meditation he arrived at this clear-cut conclusion, a sick heart is the source of the world's woe.

Note the contrast between his answer and the answer of the thinkers of the Far East. Jeremiah was an Asiatic, but there is not a trace of the Asiatic philosophy in all his thinking. He never fell under the delusion that matter is the seat of evil, or that a man's tribulations and miseries come from his body. He struck his finger on the place, and said, "Thou ailest here," and the spot indicated was the heart. The trouble, he said, is not in matter but in mind, not in the flesh but in the spirit, not in the body but in the will. The world is in darkness and misery because the human personality is diseased. "The heart is deceitful above all things and desperately sick."

Note again how far removed he is from our modern ways of thinking. We think constantly of our social machinery. Our machinery is not properly adjusted. If we could only add something to it or take something from it, then all would be well. But Jeremiah declares that the root of the trouble is not in the machinery at all. The source of human woe is the diseased heart. The mischief-maker of this world is its sin. The world darkness can be explained only by sin. The world's tragedies can be accounted for only by sin. Sin is not a mere visible act. Sin is a sort of blindness, a kind of deafness, a species of hardness or stubbornness of the will, a certain deadness of sensibility, a distressing paralysis of man's capacity to respond to a spiritual appeal. It is a subtle poison with which we are saturated. It is a lurch downward which is deeply ingrained. It is a sick heart which lies at the basis of all the world's wretchedness. It is the diseased heart which explains why men act as they do. The heart is deceitful, the most deceitful thing in the world. We are deceived sometimes by others, but we are most frequently deceived by ourself. Self-deception is the most common of all the forms of deception, and it is the deadliest of them all. Men do wrong because their heart lies to them. Their heart makes promises which are never fulfilled. It predicts things which never come to pass. It paints pictures which are only illusions. Men go astray because their own heart tells them lies. It would be impossible for men to do the foolish and wicked things which they do were they not deceived by their own heart. "Blessed is the man who trusts in God, and whose hope is in God. He shall be as a tree planted by the waters, and that spreadeth out his roots by the river, and shall not fear when heat cometh, but his leaf shall be green; and shall not be careful in the year of drought, neither shall cease from yielding fruit." If all this is true, why do men ever sin? If God blesses the good man so abundantly, why do not all men become good? If sin brings only disappointment and sorrow, why do men ever do wrong? The answer of the prophet is, "The heart is deceitful above all things, and it is desperately sick." No better answer than that has ever yet been given.

We need this man Jeremiah, for we are living in a superficial age, and we Americans are probably the most superficial of all peoples. Our superficiality is the result of the haste in which we live. We have so many interesting things to look at that we cannot look at any one thing long, not long enough to get under the skin of it. We have so many things to think about, we cannot think about anything more than a minute. We have no time to think any problem through. We have so many places to go, that we are always on the rush. We flit from place to place and dabble in this and that, and get a smattering of a hundred different kinds of knowledge, but come to know nothing

well. We need Jeremiah. We are just the people
to be hoodwinked by the notion that the social
order is responsible for our troubles. We get our
eyes on the social machinery, and we itch to give
it another twist. We are always stretching out
our hand toward Albany. We are eager to get
our hand on the legislature. We want to mold
it according to our will. If the legislature would
only do what we want it to do, then the common-
wealth would speedily recover. We stretch our
hand toward Washington city. We are crazy to
get our hand upon Congress. We are impatient
to have Congress do more than it is doing. We
have thousands of laws already, but we want more
of them. If we only had more laws, then our
troubles would be ended. If the machinery could
be readjusted, we would go forward with singing.
We are tremendously interested in legislation, in
methods, in programs, and in panaceas, we are
not greatly concerned about the heart.

Even our so-called thinkers are in appalling
numbers shallow men. They do not go to the
roots of things. These social doctors who talk
so much about Socialism and Collectivism and
Syndicalism and Communism do not ordinarily
take into account the fact and force of sin. They
ignore it. They lay their plans and leave out the
very force which will upset all their plans. They

paint pictures of a social order which can never be so long as sin blocks the way. They build lovely castles, but they build them in the air. These castles can have no foundation on the earth because of the presence of sin. Our social doctors have a genius for painting attractive pictures, but their pictures are worth nothing because they paint what can never be. Before you paint a picture of a happy world, you must settle your account with sin. You can usually measure the profundity of a thinker by his conception of sin. If any teacher makes light of sin, you may rest assured you are listening to a shallow man, a man who does not understand the world he is living in, and from whom you can expect no sound instruction.

The shallowness of our age comes to its climax in the popular view of sin. It has become almost a proverb that no sensible man worries any longer about his sins. Sin is nothing but a trifle, why should you worry about it? Sin is a sort of greenness, rawness, immaturity, awkwardness, you will outgrow it if you only wait. You are not disturbed by the awkwardness of your young children. That awkwardness will by and by disappear. So will sin vanish in the course of your growth. Sin is only a rash, an affection of the skin. It does not go down into the muscle, it does not affect the bone. It is all on the surface. An inexpensive lotion will relieve it. It will some morning vanish and leave not a scar behind. It is a pimple. It disfigures you a bit, but there is nothing dangerous about it. Why distress yourself about a pimple?

But Jeremiah nursed no such illusions. He saw that sin is a cancer, a malignant disease which goes down to the very roots of our being. He saw that there is no physician this side of God who can do anything for it. Did you ever feel the pathos of his piercing question—"Is there no balm in Gilead? Is there no physician there?" Gilead was a region which lay on the prophet's eastern horizon. It was over Gilead that the sun rose every morning to illumine little Anathoth and big Jerusalem. It was the land which symbolized hope. In Gilead grew the herbs and trees and flowers from which balsams were made to supply the physicians of that Eastern world. Is there no balm even in Gilead? Is there no physician, no prophet, no priest, no healer, no teacher who can cure a sick heart? And the answer is "No." There is no remedy on earth for a heart which is desperately sick. Did you ever catch the agony which pulses in his question, "Can the Ethiopian change his skin, or the leopard his spots?" Can the negro make his black skin white, can the leopard change the markings on his back and sides? The answer is "No." So also is it impossible for any man to change his heart.

Because the prophet saw the heinousness of sin, he shuddered at the penalty of it. The conception of sin and the conception of punishment always modify each other. Hold a shallow view of sin, and you will also hold a shallow notion of retribution. If sin is a trifle, then punishment will be only nominal. But if sin is heinous, then punishment will be awful. Jeremiah believed that sin is heinous, and therefore he was sure that punishment will be awful. He told the people that if they persisted in their sinning, their temple would be burnt, and the walls of Jerusalem would be pounded into dust, and their country would be blotted out. Of course the people did not believe him. The king despised him, the princes mocked him, the politicians sneered at him, the priests derided him, even the prophets contradicted him. They all were jaunty optimists. They fell into the popular fashion of making light of sin. They said "Peace, peace," when there was no peace. They said, to the people, "You are all right. Go ahead," when they were all wrong and were headed toward destruction. Society has reached its lowest depth when even the leaders of religion ignore or make light of sin. It all came out just as the prophet had predicted. The temple was burned, Jerusalem was razed to the ground, the people were carried off into exile. All the clever people in Jerusalem had thought that Jeremiah had painted the picture too black. That is what shallow people always think. You cannot paint the picture too black for any man or any nation who goes on trampling on the law of the Almighty.

Are we sick, then, to despair? No. Jeremiah shows us a way out. We are afflicted with an incurable disease—incurable to any earthly physician, but not incurable to God. God can cure a sick heart. He can do something more wonderful than that. He can give us a new heart. He can write his law in the heart. He can create a new man. Six hundred years after Jeremiah, Jesus of Nazareth took up this idea of a new heart, and proclaimed it with thrilling eloquence in the streets of Jerusalem and in the cities of Galilee. "You must be born again." That was his amazing declaration. When men asked him what he meant, his reply was, "I cannot explain it, no one can understand it, but I state to you the simple fact, you must be born again. You must be born from above. Unless you are born from above, you cannot enter into the Kingdom of God!"

The experience of many centuries is driving us irresistibly to the acceptance of Jeremiah's idea of sin. We are slowly learning how desperately sick the heart is, and how impossible it is to get out of our distresses save by the method which Jeremiah and Jesus have prescribed. Men used to think that the curse of curses is poverty. It is the mother of all woes. If people only had an abundance of the necessaries of life, then contentment would dwell in every home, and laughter and song would fill all the land. But the time has come when we enjoy an amazing material prosperity. We are the richest people on the earth. No other nation since time began has ever possessed so much money as we now have. The average income of our population has never been so high in any land or at any time. Our gold is piled in glittering heaps. Our wealth runs beyond all computation. And yet alas! what do your eyes behold? There is nothing so amazing to a thoughtful mind as the demonstrated impotency of money to cure any of our social ills. Abundance from sea to sea, and yet in every city tragedies which cannot be numbered or described. The heart is desperately sick, and silver and gold cannot cure it.

Men used to think that ignorance was the greatest of all earth's scourges. Men were wretched because they were ignorant, and nations languished because of their lack of knowledge. Education was the panacea prescribed by all the social doctors. We live in a land of schools. We have more schools than any other people. We have invested more money in institutions of learning than any other nation has ever invested since time began. We have more teachers and more pupils, bigger faculties and larger classes than can be found in any other country, but we are not delivered from the curses by which the race has been tormented through the ages. Our literati are in some instances degraded and debasing teachers, and our intellectuals, so-called, are too often pessimists and cynics. Go into the world of culture and you find the same vices and the same meannesses and the same enmities and jealousies and hatreds which you find in the slums. The heart is desperately sick and book learning is not able to cure it.

Through many generations men have dreamed of Utopias to be established by setting up a better governmental system. We have been tinkering at our political machinery for thousands of years. We have tried every conceivable political device. We have experimented with despotisms and dictatorships and autocracies and oligarchies and bureaucracies and monarchies of different types, and republics of various kinds, and now we are trying Democracy, government of the people, by the people and for the people, but alas! the golden age is not here. The golden age is not even in sight. We are still face to face with the persistent fact that the heart is deceitful above all things and desperately sick. Our only consolation is that which came to the prophet. Let me quote you the remainder of his sentence. He does not stop with his declaration concerning the sickness of the heart. He goes on to add something which he could hear God saying, "I search the mind, I try the heart, I reward every man according to his deeds." The prophet found relief by bringing God in. In the ninth chapter of the book, there is a paragraph which we would do well to write in our heart: "Let not the wise man glory in his wisdom, neither let the mighty man glory in his might, let not the rich man glory in his riches; but let him that glories, glory in this, that he knows God, the God who delights in exercising loving kindness and judgment and righteousness in the earth."

VIII

PRAYER IS CONVERSATION WITH GOD

Jeremiah nowhere says that in so many words. He never says anything about prayer. He touched on many interesting subjects in the course of his long life, but, so far as we know, he never dealt with the subject of prayer. He was not a theological professor. He took no interest in the rationale of prayer. He did not weigh the arguments for prayer and the objections against prayer and deduct a conclusion after the fashion of a logician. He was not an instructor in the art of praying. He was not a scientific lecturer on the structure and forms of prayer. Nor was he an exhorter to prayer. The Hebrew poets were always exhorting people to pray. "O come let us worship and bow down, let us kneel before the Lord our Maker." They were always speaking after that fashion, but there is not a trace of that in Jeremiah. He does not encourage his countrymen to pray. He was inclined to think the people of Jerusalem prayed too much. They relied too much on their praying. In his opinion they did not pray in the right way, and their prayers were for the most part futile. He came at last to feel that he himself was praying for them too much. When he prayed to God for them, he was conscious of no response. He felt that God did not want him to pray for his countrymen. He was convinced that all prayer for the safety of Jerusalem was vain, and that even if Moses, the greatest of the lawgivers, and Samuel, the greatest of the judges, should beseech God for these people, God would turn a deaf ear to their entreaties. Jeremiah was not a professional instructor in prayer, nor an exhorter to prayer, but he was one of the greatest teachers of prayer who has ever lived. There are two ways of teaching. One may teach by precept or he may teach by example. He may teach by lecturing, by definition and exposition and argument. He may hand you his idea of prayer wrapped up in the folds of a luminous sentence, or he may give you his idea of prayer simply by praying. When you hear a man pray, you have found out his idea of prayer. His prayer life imparts to you a knowledge more satisfying than any which could be conveyed in words. It is by the prayer life of Jeremiah that we learn his conception of prayer, and it is through his practice of communing with God that the Spirit exhorts us to pray. Life after all is the great teacher. As Emerson says, "Nor knowest thou what argument thy life to thy neighbor's creed hath lent."

I wonder how many of you have ever studied the prayers of Jeremiah. The chief ones are found in chapters twelve, fourteen, fifteen, seventeen, eighteen, twenty and thirty-two. We are everlastingly indebted to Baruch for writing these prayers down. All of the prayers are interesting, and some of them are surprising. We are astonished that they should have been given a place in this volume. We are amazed that a friend so loyal as Baruch, should so give away his friend as he has done by reporting some of these prayers. And moreover we are dumbfounded by the fact that Jeremiah should have told Baruch that some of these prayers ever came from his mouth. Jeremiah must have repeated them to Baruch, for otherwise Baruch could not have known what they were. And one would have supposed that a prophet would have been ashamed ever to confess that he had spoken to God after this fashion. One of the outstanding traits of the Bible is its delicious frankness. It paints its heroes, warts and all. It is the honestest book ever written. All the prayers of Jeremiah, good and bad, wise

and foolish, worthy and unworthy, are spread out
before us for our admonition and instruction and
comfort.

Jeremiah was preëminently a man of prayer.
Some of us have called him the "weeping
prophet," but there is no evidence that he ever
wept. He said on one memorable occasion that
he felt like crying, but we are not told that he
actually cried. We have indubitable proof that
he prayed. His contemporaries did not look upon
him as a weeping prophet, they revered him as
a man of prayer. The kings did not like him and
paid scant attention to what he said, but at least
one of them looked up to him as a man mighty
in prayer. At a crisis in the life of the nation,
when the sky was black and all the stars were
dead, and the government was caught in a swirl
of forces which no one was able to control, King
Zedekiah sent two officers to Jeremiah begging
him to pray for him and his people. What a
thrilling picture that is! A king driven to desperation in a great storm that threatens to overwhelm his kingdom, turns to a man whom he does
not like, and whose counsel he has repeatedly
rejected, saying, "O pray for me!" A few years
later a similar situation was again presented.
Jerusalem had fallen, the Temple and the palaces
had been burned, the influential and wealthy

people had been carried off to Babylon, only a miserable remnant was left behind. The man who had been appointed Governor over them, had been brutally assassinated, and the people were filled with confusion and terror. They did not know which way to turn or what to do. They feared the incensed King of Babylon would come back and place his mighty foot upon them and crush them all to death. In their desperation they gathered round Jeremiah. They implored him to pray for them. That is a picture not to be forgotten, a distracted and hopeless company of people headed by their impotent leaders, clinging to a man whom most of them had previously despised, crying, "O speak to God for us and find out from him what we ought to do!" Above all the other men of his generation Jeremiah was a man of prayer.

How did he become such? In the first place he was born in a prayerful home. His father was a priest, and therefore a man of prayer. The little boy Jeremiah had often listened to his father praying. He is a fortunate boy who hears his father pray. How many of you ever heard your father pray? If you never heard him in prayer, you have suffered a great loss. Jeremiah was born in a home in which there was a library. The library was not a large one when compared with

the libraries of our day, but it was a good one.
A priest could not get on without books. Some
of those books were prayer books, and little Jeremiah no doubt looked into them. A boy dips into
everything. He is sure to look into every book
which lies within his reach. Jeremiah looked into
his father's prayer books, and what he read there
helped to make him a man of prayer. Fortunate
is the boy who is born into a home which has
books in it, especially religious books which lead
the mind out and up to God.

When Jeremiah grew up his experience drove
him little by little into a particular style of praying. He did not take an interest in the ceremonial
prayers which he heard in the temple. Prayers
can be used in various ways. They can be used
as formulas, forms of pious words which are
repeated again and again by appointed leaders
or by the whole congregation as an incantation for
the purpose of securing the blessing of God. Or
they may be sung by chanting choirs as embellish-
ments of a splendid spectacle, a gorgeous and
impressive performance. But Jeremiah did not
care for the prayers in the temple. To him they
were formal and hollow. The people did not put
their hearts into them, and moreover Jeremiah
saw that they were no better men after all their
praying. And so he retired into himself. Deeper

and deeper he withdrew into his own heart. He did not pray in the temple of Solomon, he prayed in the temple of his own soul. He did this more and more because he was a lonely man. He had no wife or children. He never married because he was unwilling to subject any woman to the suffering which was certain to come to one who was linked to a man so unpopular as he was. He had no neighbors. His early neighbors in Anathoth all turned against him because he identified himself with a reform which was especially unpopular in that town. They hated him with such a venomous hatred that he had to leave his native village and make his home in Jerusalem. In that big city he had many enemies and few friends. He was ostracized by most of the best people in the city, and compelled to live a life of isolation. He found himself more and more sitting in a corner alone. He had no social life. He suffered more than tongue could tell. "Why is my pain perpetual?" was a question which often came from his anguished heart. Because he had no man to talk with he formed the habit of talking more and more with God. Driven out of human society, he lived more and more in close fellowship with the Eternal. It was in this way that prayer became to him conversation, an intimate intercourse with God. In his loneliness and

[153]

suffering he discovered that true prayer is intimate fellowship with God. This is one of the great blessings which he has bestowed upon the world. He has taught the whole human race that prayer is talking with God.

We would do well often to ponder this truth, that prayer is conversation between the soul and the infinite Father. It is because we forget this, that our praying so often becomes irksome and unrewarding. To Jeremiah, prayer was dialogue. He said something to God, and God replied. God said something to Jeremiah, and Jeremiah responded. We too often make prayer monologue. We do all the talking. A monologue is always more or less stupid. We get tired of talking alone. Nothing is more boresome than trying to hold a conversation with some one who refuses to converse.

You say something and there is a dead silence. You say something else, and there is a sound scarcely audible. You try it again but without success, and in your disgust you give up. That is why some of us have given up prayer. Our prayer was a monologue. We said something and God said nothing. We got discouraged and ceased to pray.

Prayer to Jeremiah was fellowship. He communed with God. He talked not to God but with

God. He entered into a conversation with God. There was an interplay of thought and feeling. There are people in the city to whom we speak. We know them by name and by face, and we greet them when we pass them, but we never converse with them. They hold a higher social rank than we do, and to expect them to converse with us would be on our part presumption. We speak to them but we do not expect them to converse with us. We would be willing to converse, but for them to converse with such insignificant creatures as we are, is out of the question. That is the way some of us feel about God. We can speak to him but he will not speak to us. He is God, too far above us for him to enter into a friendly intercourse with us. We speak to him, he never speaks to us. He does not do it because he is the great and Holy one, high and lifted up. This is why our prayers are oftentimes so cold. We have a distant acquaintance with God. We salute him, we pay obeisance to him, but we never converse. We are never on intimate terms.

To Jeremiah prayer was a privilege. He liked to pray. He prayed because he found joy in it. It never occurred to him that it was a duty. If he had looked upon it as a duty, he would have spoiled it all. God was his friend, and he was a friend of God, and two friends talk with one another, not because it is their duty to do it, but because it is a natural and delightful thing to do. I do not talk with my friends because it is my duty to do it. I do it solely because I like to do it. I would rather do it than almost anything else in the world. If I should say to my friend, "I am going to talk with you an hour. I feel it is my duty to do it," that would block the way to all prosperous conversation, and would ultimately put an end to our friendship itself. Friendship cannot live in the realm of duty. We talk with our friends for no other reason than because we like to do it. If you consider praying a duty, you have made progress in the prayer life impossible. Everybody who has prayed from a sense of duty ought to get rid of that idea at once. One of the most effective of all ways of killing the spontaneity and enjoyment of praying is to look upon prayer as a task which you have got to perform.

To Jeremiah, praying was easy. It was easy because it was conversation. Conversation with a friend is always easy. We never notice the passing of time when we chat with a friend. We always live above the clock when we are in the presence of those we love. We talk an hour with a friend, and then accidentally looking at the clock we exclaim, "Where has the time gone?"

It is as easy to converse as it is to breathe. But to make a speech is difficult. A speech is a technical and artistic thing. To make a good speech is an arduous achievement. One must consider his vocabulary. He must have just the right words and no others. He must be careful of his pronunciation. One cannot afford to mispronounce words in the presence of persons of culture. He must look out for his grammar and syntax. He must keep his pronouns in the right cases and his verbs in the right number. He must also pay attention to his rhetoric. The form of the sentence must be pleasing, and the sentences must follow one another in the right sequence. To make a speech is a sizeable job. One reason why some of us find it difficult to pray is because we look upon prayer as a speech, a little speech to God. We make him a speech in the morning, and another in the evening, and it becomes quite burdensome before the end of the week. It is a great bother to make so many speeches. In the morning we are so busy it is easy to forget making our speech. You have heard people say, "I forgot to say my prayers." In other words, "I forgot to make my speech to God." When you forget to say your prayers, you need not worry about it. Nothing much was lost, either for you or for God. He does not care about your little speeches, and your little speeches have no effect on your life. A prayer which is only a speech is not a part of you. It lacks reality. It is something artificial and stuck on. Prayer to be real must be conversation, an integral part of life. Conversing with a friend is natural and exhilarating. I heard a woman many years ago say that she would be so glad when she got to heaven, because there she would not have to pray any more. Poor woman! She had been making speeches for many years, one in the morning and one in the evening, and she was all tired out. She looked forward to heaven as a city of refuge to which she could flee after death, in order to escape from the clutches of the awful duty of praying. Many persons never find sufficient courage to pray in public, and the chief reason is that to them prayer is a beautiful speech. They cannot make a speech in public!

The prayers of Jeremiah were varied and therefore always fresh. They were never stale or monotonous. How to keep prayer from becoming tedious and repetitious is a problem with which many of us have wrestled. We find ourselves saying the same old things over and over again. Jeremiah had no such trouble because prayer in his view was conversation, the communion of the soul with God. We are handicapped, I fear, by certain assumptions which are ruinous to all freedom and gladness in praying. We imagine that whenever we speak to God, we must begin by thanking him for his goodness to us. Who made such a rule? Jeremiah knew nothing of it, nor did Jesus of Nazareth. Jesus did not thank God every time he spoke to him. He did not thank him, for instance, in the garden of Gethsemane, nor did he thank him in any one of his three recorded prayers on the cross. When he taught his disciples the general spirit of efficacious prayer, he did not include any expression of thanksgiving. When we repeat the so-called Lord's Prayer, we do not strike the note of gratitude. This does not mean that we are never to thank God. Jesus often thanked him, and so shall we if we pray in the spirit of Jesus, but we shall not thank God every time we speak to him. Try to impose such a rule in the home! Tell a boy that he must never speak to his father without beginning by thanking him for being so good to him. The boy would pay no attention to such preposterous advice. He has too much common sense for that. If he tried it, his father would be bored. You put an end to all normal and healthy conversation if you load it down with mechanical rules. Anything artificial or stereotyped destroys the sweetness and gladness of intercourse between father and son. Some of us assume we must confess our sins to God every time we approach him. Jeremiah knew nothing of such a requirement, nor did Saul of Tarsus. They often confessed their sins, but not always. There are times when confession is natural and wholesome, but to make confession a part of every prayer is absurd. Command a boy never to speak to his father without telling him what a bad boy he has been, and you take away all desire from the boy to meet his father at all. Moreover, you weary the father by foisting on him a story which he does not want everlastingly to hear. The story becomes all the more fatiguing to him if it is a confession already made many times of sins committed long ago. We weary God with our multiplied and automatic confessions.

Would you avoid monotony in your praying? Think of prayer as conversation. We are never troubled by monotony when we are conversing with our friends. When we meet a friend, we do not say, "What did we talk about the last time we met? Let us say it all over again." We begin at once on something recent and vital. "What have you been doing?" That is one of the first questions always. Friends who have been separated for awhile always are eager to know what has been happening to each of them in their absence one from the other. Or if they do not talk about the immediate past, they devote themselves to the immediate future. "What are you going to do this summer?" Already I hear you asking one another that question. When we compare notes with our friends in regard to what we have been doing, or what we are going to do, we are never plagued by monotony. Why not make prayer conversation with God? Why not every morning talk over with him the things you are going to do? We have our plan for the day. Why not discuss it with him? We expect to meet certain persons, to do certain bits of work, to grapple with certain problems, to deal with certain situations, and why not talk with God about them at the beginning of the day? If we do this, prayer can never become monotonous, for no two days are alike. Every day has its own duties and experiences, and if we talk with God about the passing day, we always have something new to talk about, something of interest to us, and therefore of interest to him. At the close of the day, why not talk over with him the things we have done? Various things have happened and why not talk with him about them? We failed here and there, we succeeded in this or that, we did good and maybe we did harm, we said things perhaps which

we should not have said, or we did things which
it was not wise to do, and all these matters are
proper subjects for the evening conversation with
God. Things happened to us. We met with
interruptions or delays or disappointments or a
misfortune or possibly a sorrow, and all these
may profitably be pondered in the presence of
God. We had an experience which we did not
understand. Something happened which we were
unable to explain. All mysteries are best dealt
with in conversation with God. There is nothing
monotonous in talking over a day with God.

How did Jeremiah learn this wisdom? It came
to him through his humble heart. We get a
revelation of the man's innermost nature in the
first chapter of the Book. Did you ever notice
that the Book opens with a prayer, a dialogue
between Jeremiah and God? Jeremiah is a young
man and is struggling with the question of his
life work. He is not sure what he wants to do,
or what he ought to do, or what he is best fitted
for. It is a solemn period in any man's career
when he is making up his mind what he is going
to do the remainder of his life. A mistake at this
point may be fatal. Many a man wrestles with
the problem in an agony of bloody sweat. Jeremiah was passing through this ordeal. He felt
sometimes that he ought to be a prophet, or as

we would say, a preacher, he ought to enter the
ministry. But at other times, he felt that the
ministry was no place for him. He was not fitted
for it. He could not succeed in it. He talked
the matter over with God. God told him he
wanted him to be a prophet, and Jeremiah told
God he could not be one because he could not
speak. How can a man be a preacher if he has
not the gift of speech? He went on to tell God
how inexperienced he was. "I am just a child."
In that expression, "I am a child," we see deep
into this man's soul. He was always a child. To
the end of his life he remained a child. He never
grew up. He had the naïveté and abandon and
audacity of a child. He is the most childlike man
in the Bible with the single exception of Jesus of
Nazareth. His childlikeness comes out more
clearly in his prayers than in any other department
of his life.

He was always asking questions. His prayers
bristle with interrogation points. To him the
world was a constant puzzle, and Jeremiah was
continually asking for explanations. Things were
always happening to him which puzzled him. He
asked God what they meant. He had experiences
which he could not understand, and he went to
God for light. Some of us do not ask God questions. Asking questions of God seems to us some-

[163]

what impertinent. We ask men questions but not God. But if God is our father, why should we not ask him questions? It is a child's right to ask questions. It is by asking questions that the child grows. Nothing is more unwise in a parent than to discourage his children in asking questions. God, no doubt, likes to have us ask him questions, and we should carry all our hardest ones to him in prayer. There are times when the only prayer we can offer is a question.

He was always ready to give God information in regard to what was going on. It was his habit to tell God all about himself, and about what he was doing and thinking and feeling. He poured out his innermost heart before God. He also told God what his enemies were doing and saying, and he told him how he was suffering, and what ugly feelings he had toward the men who were treating him with such cruelty and meanness. He did only what every child does. A child tells his parents a lot of things which his parents already know. It is his right to do this. It opens up his nature. It creates new bonds of sympathy and understanding. It assists the child in his development. These wiseacres who inform us oracularly that we ought not to tell God anything which he already knows, think they are clever, but in fact they are both

[164]

ignorant and stupid. They do not know the A,
B, C's of life. They understand neither God
nor the soul, nor the way in which the soul grows
in God. If you insist that we shall not tell God
anything he knows, you so impoverish prayer that
prayer ultimately becomes impossible.

Jeremiah had all the boldness of a child. He
blurted out things to God which shock us. He
sometimes chided God, scolded him, reprimanded
him, told him he was not giving him a fair deal.
One day he cried out, "O God, you have deceived
me! You have gotten me into this horrible
predicament, and now refuse to help me out!"
This is a new note in the history of religion, this
bold and intimate speaking to God. In talking
in this style, Jeremiah was taking the liberty of
a child. Did you ever see a little child strike his
mother? She did something he did not like, and
instantly he doubled up his little fist and struck
her. What did she do? Did she resent it and
say, "I'll make you smart for that! I'll remember
that the longest day I live." She said nothing
of the sort. That little fist did not hurt her. She
knew the tantrum would speedily pass away. She
did not resent the blow because he was her child.
He belonged to her. The feeble blow of the tiny
fist only drew her more closely to him. We do

[165]

not say harsh things to God to his face. Some of us, however, talk about him behind his back. We have the very feelings which Jeremiah had but we do not express them in our prayers. Some of us feel we have not been fairly treated. We have been denied a square deal. We have never had our share of the good things in the world. All around us are men and women, no better than we are, or wiser or abler or more deserving, who have had a hundred times more given to them than we have received. We have been treated shabbily. We do not say that in our prayers, but we carry it in our heart. Some of us feel we have had more than our share of trouble. We have had losses one after the other, and sorrows, heart-breaking sorrows. We have been overtaken by misfortunes and calamities which have never come to our neighbors and friends. There is no justice in the way in which God has treated us. We do not say this to God in our prayers, but we say it to ourselves behind his back. It is better to speak all such feelings out in our prayers. Why should we not tell God to his face that we think he has treated us meanly and has never given us a fair chance to enjoy life as we had a right to enjoy it? Jeremiah got nearer to God because of his frankness. God came nearer to him because Jeremiah was such a simple-hearted and honest child. Jesus of Nazareth, the most childlike man who has ever lived, used to say, "Except you become as a little child, you shall in no wise enter into the Kingdom of Heaven." It is equally true that unless we become as little children, we can never enter into the liberty and joy of praying.

IX

LOYALTY TO GOD IS ABOVE LOYALTY TO THE GOVERNMENT

You will not find this sentence anywhere in the Book of Jeremiah, and yet it expresses one of his cardinal convictions. He was not a professor of political philosophy. He did not lecture on the duties of citizenship. He was not interested in the relation of religion to politics or of the church to the state. No such questions had come up at that time. He was not an instructor in the virtue of patriotism. He never expounded the nature of patriotism or attempted to lay down the obligations of the patriot.

He was a speaker but he was still more a doer. He was the star actor on a crowded stage at one of the great crises in the history of the world. He taught men by his tongue, but he taught them still more effectively by his life. Actions, they say, speak louder than words. The actions of Jeremiah, are trumpet-tongued. A man's dominant ideas come out in his deeds. You find out what a man believes by watching what he does. One of the ideas which he proclaimed in a voice of thunder, thunder which has been reverberating in the ears of men through seventy-five generations, and which will continue to reverberate down to the last syllable of recorded time, is the idea that loyalty to God takes precedence over loyalty to the government. Edith Cavell said in our day, "Patriotism is not enough." Jeremiah said the same thing twenty-five hundred years ago.

I am going to lead you into a dark and perilous region of thought, a region containing many pitfalls, and where the air is filled with blinding mists. It is a country infested by many puzzling and vexing questions, and one is met at every turn by teasing and baffling problems. The problems demand a deal of patient and serious thinking, more thinking than they have as yet received. Some persons have not thought of them at all, others have thought about them just enough to become bewildered by them, those who have thought about them most have not been able to arrive at the same conclusions. Wherever you travel in this dimly lighted region, you carry in your ears the discord of clashing opinions. It behooves us therefore to proceed with deliberation and to begin with a few definitions and by pointing out sundry distinctions which are sometimes overlooked. In dealing with complex and provocative subjects, we do well to agree at the beginning on the meaning of the terms we are going to use.

Notice first of all the phrasing of our subject. "Loyalty to God is above loyalty to the government." Mark it is the "government" not the "country." It is popularly assumed that the country and the government are one and the same thing. Loyalty to the government and loyalty to the nation are counted identical. But this is a false assumption. The country and the government are two different things.

What is our country? First of all, it is a wide strip of land, an area of over three million square miles. We spread our hand over the map of the United States and we say proudly, "That is my country." "I love thy rocks and rills, thy woods and templed hills"—that is the way we sing. "Our heart with rapture thrills, like that above." But our country is more than millions of square miles of land. It is the people who live on the land. There are one hundred and twenty million people, they are our countrymen. We belong to them, and we are proud of them. But our country is more than the people. It is the whole mass of principles and traditions and institutions which have come out of these people, and which are revered by them and sustained by them. Our country is the sum total of our homes and our schools and our churches and our political tribunals through which the will of the people finds expression. Everything under the flag—that is our country.

What is the government? It is the group of men who at any particular time are invested with political authority. They are the company of politicians who have climbed to the seats of political power. They are the committee to whom has been committed the responsibility of molding political policies and framing political programs. The government is the ruling group in the country.

The country changes slowly and imperceptibly, but the government changes rapidly and all the time. It changes continuously in its personnel. Men are coming and going constantly. One set passes out of office, another comes in. One party is succeeded by another party, and with the change of party comes a change of policy and program. In England a Tory government is succeeded by a Liberal government, and that by a Labor government, and that by a Coalition government. In the United States the Democratic party gives way to the Republican party, and the Republican party is succeeded by the Democratic party. For years the Democratic party holds control of the government. But one day Abraham Lincoln is elected, and the new president brings with him a new set of men and a new set of ideas. Theodore Roosevelt brings with him to Washington a set of men pledged to a particular policy, and when Woodrow Wilson comes in he brings with him a different following with different policies to be established.

It comes about then that a man may be the friend of his country but not the friend of the government, he may sympathize with his country while he has no sympathy with his government. It is not hard for an American to make this distinction, because our fathers made it at the very beginning of their political career. They loved their country, but they hated their government. Their government was British with its headquarters on the other side of the Atlantic, and because they were such ardent lovers of their country, they despised their government. One of their leaders wrote down in language which has become immortal the declaration that there are a few inalienable rights which belong to human beings, and that whenever the government fails to secure for the people these rights, then it is the duty of the people to alter it or abolish it and set up another government which seems likely to secure the results desired.

It is because the distinction between one's country and one's government is so frequently lost sight of, that we have such clashing statements concerning patriotism. Some people eulogize patriotism, as one of the highest of all the virtues, while others spurn patriotism as a curse. Several years ago, I made a collection of the opinions of a few distinguished thinkers in regard to the matter, and I was surprised at the harshness of the language they used. Ruskin asserted that patriotism is an absurd prejudice. Grant Allen declared that it is a vulgar vice. Havelock Ellis contended that it is a virtue among barbarians. Herbert Spencer condemned it as "extended selfishness." Leo Tolstoi was especially severe saying that it is "an unnatural, irrational and harmful feeling, and should be suppressed and eradicated by all means available to rational men." That is not quite so drastic as the judgment of Samuel Johnson, who declared in his Dictionary that "patriotism is the last refuge of a scoundrel."

Why do men speak after this fashion? They confuse loyalty to the country with loyalty to the government. They are wide readers of history, and they know what havoc so-called patriotism has wrought. Men have been loyal to their government no matter how wild and wicked their government has been. In their desire to be patriotic, they have followed their government into stupid and abominable courses, and have brought on their country unspeakable disasters. Devotion to government has been everything which these writers have pictured it. It has been a vulgar vice, an atrocious exhibition of selfishness, an irrational and destructive fanaticism. But this devotion to government is not patriotism. True patriotism is love of one's country, and that is always a beautiful and a noble thing.

> Breathes there a man with soul so dead,
> Who never to himself hath said,
> This is my own, my native land!

Patriotism is a fire, a sacred fire. It burns in the hearts of men in every land, and will burn on forever. It can never be extinguished because it is kindled at the heart of God. Loyalty to God is above, not loyalty to one's country, but loyalty to one's government.

Let us now turn to the expression, "Loyalty to God." That is a pious sounding conventional phrase, but what does it mean? Who is God and what is God? To many the name "God" is merely a glorified word which stands for the incomprehensible. One of the honestest men of our day has confessed that to him God has always been "an oblong blur." To many the word "God" is only a symbol standing for an indefinite something that nobody knows anything about. Let us try to put a definite ascertainable meaning into the phrase. Let us substitute another word for the word "God," not a completely adequate word, but a word which suggests the meaning of God and approximates it. Let us try the word "truth." God, we are told is a God of truth. Christ said, "I am the truth." Since Christ is the image of God, then God is the truth. To be loyal to the truth is to be loyal to God. No one can be loyal to God who is not loyal to the truth. Or try another word, "right." We read in the Bible of the God of Righteousness. Christ is our righteousness. Righteousness is a long word for rightness, and rightness is a long word for right. Loyalty to God means loyalty to the right. A man who is not loyal to the right cannot be loyal to God. Or try another word, "wisdom." God is infinitely wise. He is a God of wisdom. Christ is the wisdom of God. To be loyal to God is to be loyal to wisdom. Our proposition now reads, "Loyalty to truth and right and wisdom is above loyalty to the government."

At this point a difficulty emerges. What is

truth? What is right? What is wisdom? Men do not agree. The Christian Scientist reads the book of Mrs. Mary Baker Eddy and feels he is reading the truth. We do not think he is. We think he is getting a smattering of the truth, a grain of the truth, a grain of truth now and then, but certainly not the full-orbed truth. The Latter Day Saint reads the book of Mormon and says the manner of life here set forth is right. We read the book and say, "All this is wrong." The Confucianist reads the Analects of his Teacher and says, "These express the highest wisdom." But we toss aside this maxim and that, saying, "That is not wise." And so we must now introduce another word, "conscience." A man must follow his conscience or moral judgment. He has his own conception of what is true and right and wise, and this is the conception by which he is to live. Loyalty to God, therefore, is loyalty to conscience, and our sentence now reads, "Loyalty to conscience is above loyalty to the government."

Theoretically we all agree to this. Who would dare deny it? We may not be willing to live up to it ourself, but we admire men who do. Jesus did it, and he would not be our Savior if he had not done it. We cannot think of him putting Galilee above truth, or Judea above right, or Palestine above wisdom, or Caesar above God.

He put God above everything and above everybody, everywhere and always. When we hear him say to Pontius Pilate, "To this end was I born, and for this cause came I into the world, to bear witness to the truth," we feel a thrill in the heart, knowing we have heard something high and fine.

The Apostles followed Jesus' example. When they were arrested in Jerusalem and commanded by the Supreme Court to say nothing further about Jesus of Nazareth, their swift reply was, "Whether it be right in the sight of God to hearken unto you rather than unto God, you may judge; but as for us our course is settled, we propose to go right on declaring the things which we have seen and heard." Again a thrill goes through our hearts. That is the kind of men we reverence. If the Apostles had said anything less than that, they would not have sat on thrones teaching all the generations.

The Christians during the first three centuries were compelled to decide again and again whether or not they should place their conscience above the Government. It was a law that all people under the Roman government should burn incense to Caesar. Burning incense was a form of worship. But the Christians would not worship Caesar: they worshiped Christ and Christ only.

They paid the penalty. They were jailed, beaten, tortured, many of them died a horrible death. But we rejoice in their death. We are proud of Polycarp speaking to us out of the flames which consumed him in Smyrna. We are proud of Perpetua in her fatal struggle with the wild beasts in the amphitheater in Carthage. We repeat with swelling hearts the adage, "The blood of the martyrs is the seed of the church." So it was. If Christians had not put loyalty to conscience above the Government, Christianity would never have gotten its grip on the world. Christianity would have died in its cradle had not Christians placed God above the Government.

In every generation, Christians have had to make the choice between obeying their conscience and obeying their rulers. Martin Luther at the Diet of Worms gives us a most vivid example. He was a prisoner compelled to answer the charges made against him. He had spoken and written certain things which had given offense to the authorities. He was ordered to recant. The Emperor was there and his retinue. The magnates of the various German states were there. High representatives of the Roman Church were there, and the reformer was commanded to take back certain things which he had written. His reply was, "Show me that I am mistaken, convince me that I am wrong, in anything which I have written, and I will retract it." But they could not show him that he was wrong. Hour after hour the struggle continued, and at the end, this is what he said, "Here I stand. I can do nothing else. God help me. Amen!" We protestants glory in the attitude and courage of Luther. We feel that the world entered on a new era when that intrepid German dared to place truth above all the governments of Europe. Theoretically we assent to the proposition that loyalty to conscience is above loyalty to the government.

But as soon as we begin to apply the principle to our own situation, we find ourselves involved in perplexities and difficulties. What do we Americans owe to our government? Have we a right to criticize it, or condemn it, or denounce it whenever it does anything which we consider foolish or wrong? Is it right to criticize the mayor? We all do it. Is it right to condemn the governor? Most of us do it. Is it right to denounce the House of Representatives or the Senate? Many of us do it. But how about criticizing the president of the United States? Many feel we ought to keep our tongue off of him. And how about the Supreme Court? Will you judge the judges of our highest tribunal? Will you dissent from a decision rendered by our highest court, and pro-

test against their expressed wisdom? Many feel
that silence at this point is a duty. But how about
the War Department and the Navy Department? Will you criticize their plans and condemn
their programs and denounce their theories?
Some say you are disloyal if you set yourself
against the counsel of the military and naval experts of the nation. This is the ark of our safety
and you are a dangerous citizen if you place your
sacrilegious hand upon that ark. In the realm
of thought and speech, will you set your conscience
above your government? Most of us answer
"yes." We claim the right to criticize and pass
judgment on every department of our government
from the bottom to the top. I presume that is
the conviction of a great majority of all the American people now alive. We claim the right to put
our conscience in thought and speech above our
government.

But how about action? Have we a right to
act against the government whenever our conscience tells us the government is asking something which it is foolish or wrong for us to do?
If the government assesses an unjust tax, shall
we smother our conscience and pay the tax?
Henry Thoreau refused to pay a tax and went to
jail for his refusal. Do you commend him?
John Clifford, one of the most popular and noble

of all English preachers of our generation was
haled into court again and again, and fined, because he refused to pay a tax which he considered
unjust. Is such conduct commendable?

Many years ago we had on our statute book,
a federal law known as the "Fugitive Slave Law."
By that law all runaway slaves were to be returned
to their legal masters, and all loyal citizens were
ordered to assist in the execution of the law. But
throughout the North there were groups of conscientious people who felt that this law was iniqui-
tous, and instead of helping to bring the runaway
slaves back to their owners, they assisted them
to get still farther away. In defiance of the law
they railroaded runaway slaves from one point
to another until they were finally landed in Can-
ada. Was that a right thing to do? Was it
Christian? Had those abolitionists a right to put
their conscience above the government?

In October 1859 John Brown gathered about
him a group of men who attacked the United
States' arsenal at Harper's Ferry. The arsenal
was captured, the guns were seized with the expectation of putting them into the hands of the
slaves who might thus fight their way to liberty.
John Brown was arrested and within two months
he was hanged. But there were groups of people
in various parts of the North who were grieved

over his death, and began to sing, at first quietly and then loudly, "John Brown's body lies amoldering in the grave, but his soul goes marching on." Was that a proper song to sing? Would you have sung it if you had been living then?

Take a suppositional law. Suppose the Federal Government should some day vote to suppress all parochial schools and compel all Roman Catholic children to go into schools provided by the government. Thousands of Roman Catholics would undoubtedly disobey the law. Would they be traitors in their disobedience? Or suppose the Federal Government should some day make military drill compulsory in all the colleges and high schools and grammar schools, and suppose thousands of boys should refuse to take the drill, and suppose their parents should back them up in their disobedience, what would you think of that form of disloyalty? The principle of putting the conscience above government seems at first sound, but is it? What do you think?

The question becomes increasingly perplexing the further you carry it. It embarrasses us in time of peace, but it is far more dubious in time of national excitement and threatened danger. When war is at the door and the majority of the people seem to be in favor of war, and the Government is on the point of declaring war, what is the good

citizen to do? Shall he put his conscience above
the people and the government? Edmund Burke
did it. Right in the midst of the American
Revolution he took the part of the Colonists and
condemned his government for its policy. John
Bright did it. He opposed Britain's entry into
the Crimean War and never hesitated to declare
his condemnation. David Lloyd George did it.
He resisted the movement to carry Britain into
the Boer War, and by doing this made himself
the most hated Welshman alive. In the year
1914, when the British Government was ponder-
ing the question whether or not to unite with
France against Germany, what did Ramsay Mac-
Donald do? And after the decision was made,
what did John Morley do? He resigned from
the cabinet because he would have nothing to do
with the administration of the war. Was it right
for John Morley at that critical hour to refuse
to give his government the advantage of his wisdom and the assistance of his wonderful brain?

But the question becomes still more puzzling
and baffling when war has been declared and the
government proceeds to draft its young men.
It treats them as slaves, lays its hand on them,
dresses them, feeds them, drills them, orders them
from one place to another, sends them to the
front, commands them to fight, to kill as many

men as possible before they themselves are killed. But suppose a man does not believe it right to go into war. He believes it is wrong to kill men even on the battlefield. He has a sensitive conscience, and to him his conscience is the voice of God. His government orders him to kill. His conscience commands him not to kill. What shall he do? Which comes first—loyalty to conscience or loyalty to the government? In the last war we had many conscientious objectors, hundreds in this country and thousands in England. What to do with them was one of the war's most perplexing problems. These men were easily jailed because they were so few in number. But their number will increase. In the next war, if the next war comes, there will be thousands of conscientious objectors to every one in the late war. There are multitudes of men who were engaged in the World War who have taken a vow before God that they will never fight again. In England over one hundred thousand men have signed a paper in which they declare that never again will they take part in any war no matter what its alleged causes may be. That paper has already been laid before the Prime Minister, and the British Government can never say it has not received warning as to what is going to happen if a next war is declared. In our own country there are small groups of men

who have made a similar pledge, never to fight in
any war, no matter what the Government may
say or do. This sentiment is evidently growing.
What is going to become of us if in time of
national danger men flatly refuse to fight? Is
the principle of placing conscience above the government a sound one? What do you think?

But the climax of perplexity is reached when
we come to deal with men over fifty who in time
of war hamper the Government in its conduct of
affairs by their speeches and writings. Some of
them are defeatists, always predicting disaster.
Others are chronic critics, breaking down morale
both in the army and in the people by their dis-
couraging and condemnatory words. The man
who breaks down morale is the most dangerous
man with whom the government has to deal.
What shall it do with a man who, impelled by
his conscience, feels it to be his duty to thwart
his government in every way he can?

These are interesting questions to-day, and
some of them are critical. They will be more
critical in the early future. These questions are
practical, and they will become more and more
puzzling as the world goes on. Our children
must face them and our grandchildren. They
will find them more urgent and daunting than
they have ever been to us. We are living in an

era of nationalism. A tremendous emphasis is placed to-day on the nation. Every nation has become self-conscious and is insistent on its rights, zealous for its interests, jealous for its honor and passionately ambitious for its place in the sun. In many quarters patriotism is a fanatical devotion to the nation, a sort of religion. The flag is made a fetish and men bow down and worship it. The prestige and power of the nation are steadily increasing. The expansion of governmental authority is one of the most startling phenomena of our time. Government is doing more and more and is steadily encroaching on the rights of the individual. In our own country we have seen government go into the business of education on the most lavish scale. Once we had only primary and grammar schools supported by the government, but now we have high schools and city colleges and great state universities. The government has become the supreme educator and also the great philanthropist. The government takes care of the orphans and the sick and the blind and the insane. We have homes and sanitoriums and asylums and institutions of many sorts and names, all supported by the government. Government has not yet gone largely into business, but it has spread out its hand over business in the most amazing manner. The governmental control over business to-day would have been deemed incredible thirty years ago. There are some who would like to see government go into business, the shipbuilding business for instance, and the coal business and the farming business. Before the World War, there was a steady trend toward the nationalization of the economic life of peoples. The movement had gone farther in Germany than in any other country. Germany had her government railroads and telegraphs and telephones, and other utilities. She subsidized her steamship companies, and in all her schools she directed education to a specific end—the exaltation of the State. And now this spirit of nationalism has taken on still more radical forms. In Russia there is a Communist State in which everything has passed over under government control. The family and the school and the press and the industries have all been taken over by the State, and there is no liberty for anybody beyond the meager privileges which the State is willing to concede. In Italy Nationalism has taken on a somewhat different form. It is known there as "Fascism." Fascism is autocracy. The State heads up in one man, a supreme dictator. Mussolini controls everything. He has blown out the flames of liberty kindled by Garibaldi and Cavour, and holds all the kingdoms of Italian life in his own mighty hand. He has brought Italy back to the despotism of the early empire.

What effect is all this going to have on religion? What is going to become of the church? In Germany before the war the church was muzzled. It had nothing to say on political programs or policies. In Moscow the church has been crowded off the sidewalk into the gutter. There is no room for religion in the Soviet State. In Italy the problem is somewhat different, for the reason that the Roman Catholic Church is a mightier institution than is the Greek Church. Things can be done in Moscow which cannot be done just yet in Rome. But in theory Fascism has no respect for the church and no place for religion. The State is the only institution deserving of men's reverence—so Fascism asserts—and every citizen is to live and move and have his being in the State. In our own country the clash has not yet come, but it is coming. There is an American nationalism which is suspicious of the church and hostile to religion. There are groups of men who are impatient with preachers who touch on governmental problems, and who denounce all churches which express an opinion in regard to programs laid down by State officials. In certain circles a clergyman is denounced as an impertinent busybody who takes an interest in any national question or is denounced as a traitor if he dissents from any opinion expressed by the officers of the navy or army. There are ominous whisperings and mutterings here and there throughout the country, and the church is destined to engage in a desperate struggle for the maintenance of its liberties and rights.

It is for this reason that the Book of Jeremiah is just now of especial worth and importance. No other book in the Bible has so much help to give us just now as this ancient Hebrew volume. It is full of suggestion to every man who is awake to the needs of mankind, and has admonition and instruction and inspiration for all who are concerned with the building of a better world.

Jeremiah was from first to last in politics. His religion drove him into politics. He could not have understood the value of any religion which would permit a man to hold aloof from the political life of his country. He was especially interested in the foreign policy of his country. That is always the most critical and important department of politics, and to that department Jeremiah devoted the full strength of his powers. He was not only a student of the policy of the Government, but a critic of it. He condemned it because he was sure it was unwise. It would lead, he declared, to disaster. It was wrong and therefore God was against it. For thirty years he kept on speaking words of warning. He exhorted the government to take heed. He remonstrated with the king. This man did not hesitate to differ from his king, or to tell the king to his face that he was pursuing a course which would lead to destruction. He opposed the ideas of the princes, the cabinet of the king. He had no confidence in their diplomacy, and he denounced and rejected their political ideas. He resisted the politicians who were a coterie of reckless jingoes, a bunch of hundred-percenters, who were always chattering about national honor, and knew nothing of national wisdom. He defied with his whole might popular opinion, and made himself the most detested man in the land. No man can oppose the opinions of the rulers and the prejudices of the masses without paying a high price. What can one man do in resisting the bent of a nation set on fire by a chauvinistic patriotism? Judah rushed on blindly to her doom. The war came. Jerusalem was besieged. Jeremiah advised the king to surrender. He urged him to give Jerusalem up. But how could the king do that? What king can surrender his capital and retain the respect of his subjects? The king refused to surrender and so Jerusalem was captured. The king's sons were brought out and killed one after another before him. His eyes were then put out, he was loaded with chains, and carried off to the City of Babylon to lie in prison till the day of his death. Jeremiah had put loyalty to God above loyalty to his king.

When the king refused to surrender, Jeremiah exhorted the soldiers not to fight. He besought them to desert. That was a daring thing to do. That was plain treason. Treason is giving aid and comfort to the enemy, and that is what Jeremiah did. Why did he do it? He did it because of his love for his countrymen. He knew what war was. He knew that it meant famine and then pestilence and then the destruction of the city by fire. He knew the city would be looted, and that thousands would be massacred, and that the palaces and the temple would be burned, and so he urged the soldiers not to fight. He made himself of no reputation, and took upon himself the form of a traitor, and became obedient unto death. The government condemned him to die. What else could it do? He was a traitor and by the law of all nations a traitor must die. Jeremiah was condemned to die. The war party would not however take his life. They would shed no blood. They feared that drops of blood would get on their hands, and that the "damned spots" would not out. And so they decided to starve him to death. They tossed him into an old cistern with a foot of mud at the bottom of it. There they left him to die.

He was a traitor, and at the same time he was a patriot. He loved his country so passionately he was willing to die for it as a traitor. He loved his country so intensely that he would not leave it even after Jerusalem was in ruins. He was offered the chance to go to Babylon, but he refused. He wanted to die in Judah. He wanted to end his days in the country in which he had been born. He wanted to live to the end under the old Palestinian stars, where he could see every morning the hills of Gilead glorious in the light of dawn, and could meditate with old Lebanon, covered in white, looking on. There was no country for him but Judah. When after the murder of the governor, the remnant of the people started to go down into Egypt, Jeremiah begged them not to go. "O let us stay in Judah." That is the last advice he ever gave them. He loved his country. He loved its rocks and rills, its groves and templed hills, his heart with rapture thrilled like that above.

He was never understood in life, but after he was dead, God took his character and showed its beauty to his countrymen. Little by little Jeremiah became a national hero. Fathers talked to their sons about him. Prophets and priests pondered his words and studied his deeds. Generals in time of war thought about him and were strengthened by him. One of the greatest of the generals in a midnight hour, dreamed about him, and in his sleep saw him coming toward him bringing help. Whenever the fortunes of the nation were at lowest ebb, the thoughts of men went out to Jeremiah, and there grew up gradually among the people the expectation that the prophet would come back again. And so when six hundred years after the prophet's death, Jesus of Nazareth appeared in Galilee producing a marvelous effect on the minds and hearts of the people, men began to say to one another, "He has come again; this is Jeremiah!"

X

THERE IS ALWAYS LIGHT AHEAD

I want to think with you to-day about Jeremiah as the prophet of hope; not a prophet of hope but the prophet who stands head and shoulders above all his fellow prophets in his genius for hoping. You may feel like challenging such a statement because the world has long considered Jeremiah as the prophet of despair. All the artists have painted him with hopeless eyes, and the popular imagination has long pictured him as a man with a desponding heart. Few men have been so widely misunderstood. For centuries he has been called the "Weeping Prophet," but there is no sound reason for giving him such a title. Some one long ago threw at him that adjective "weeping," and it has stuck to him like a burr. It is difficult to see how he will ever shake it off.

For many generations he has been credited with the authorship of the five chapters of poetry known as the Lamentations, which chapters are bound up in our Bible between the Books of Jeremiah and Ezekiel. But there is no sound reason for thinking that he wrote these poems. If you should pick up some day a Hebrew Bible you would find that the Book of Lamentations is placed between Ruth and Ecclesiastes, and you would find also that the name of Jeremiah is not attached to the book. The book has for its title simply Lamentations. This proves that at the time when the canon of the Old Testament was fixed, no one knew who wrote the Lamentations, for had the author been known, his name would have gone down in the title.

In the third century before the Christian era—three hundred years after Jeremiah's death—a company of seventy Jewish scholars translated the Old Testament into Greek. This translation is known as the "Septuagint," from the Latin word meaning seventy. In that Greek translation the Book of Lamentations was ascribed to Jeremiah, just why no one knows, and probably no one will ever find out. In the fourth century after Christ, a distinguished scholar translated the Old Testament into Latin. That translation is known as the "Vulgate." It is so called because it passed into common use in the entire Latin church. Jerome in his translation was guided by the Septuagint to ascribe the Lamentations to Jeremiah.

All our English versions of the Old Testament have been deeply influenced by the Vulgate and the Septuagint, and that explains why you read in your English Bible the title, "The Lamentations of Jeremiah." But there is no conclusive reason for believing he ever wrote the Lamentations, and there are several excellent reasons for feeling pretty sure that he never wrote one of them. But it is difficult to see how the name of Jeremiah will ever be divorced from the Book of Lamentations. Jonah and the whale will never be separated, nor is it likely that Jeremiah will ever get away from the Lamentations.

It is a fact that the prophetic volume of Jeremiah is a somber book. But that is the misfortune of Jeremiah and not his fault. He lived in a gloomy time. The time was out of joint. He tried to set it right, but he did not succeed. No one could have succeeded. The book is a long-drawn tragedy. A storm rages from the first page to the last, a storm more furious and more pitiless than the storm in King Lear. This storm beat down upon the prophet's head.

For these various reasons Jeremiah's name has become a synonym for pessimist. If at any time any of our friends becomes unduly lugubrious or doleful, we say to him contemptuously, "you are a Jeremiah!" We have taken his name and converted the last letter of it into a "d," thus coining a word which means complaint, and whenever we are bored by a hard luck story or made weary by a blubbering tirade we say that we are listening to a "jeremiad." And thus does the prophet become a symbol of gloom and stand in our memory as the incarnation of despair. It is the purpose of this sermon to wash this blot from his reputation, and to hold him up before you as the man who, with a solitary exception, had a greater genius for hoping than any man who ever lived.

It is our superficial reading of the Bible which gets us into error. The most of us read the Bible superficially as we read everything else. We skim the newspaper. It is so big there is nothing else for us to do. We skim the magazines, just a few of them. We skim a novel now and then. Few read a novel through. We skim the Bible. We skim the newspaper in the morning when we are wide-awake. We skim the Bible in the evening—if we skim it at all—when we are tired and sleepy. That is one reason why we get so little out of the Bible.

Now on the surface of it, there is no doubt the Book of Jeremiah is a pessimistic bit of literature. The gist of the book, if you read it superficially, is that the Temple is going to be burned, the City of Jerusalem is going to be demolished, the nation of Judah is going to be broken to pieces and the fragments scattered broadcast. It is a book of direful predictions. It is a book of doom. The Temple is going to be burned and nothing can prevent it. The city is going to be destroyed and nothing can save it. The people are going to be dragged into captivity and no one can rescue them. It is a picture painted in hues of midnight and eclipse. The Temple is going up in smoke. The city is going to the dogs. The nation is going to the devil. There is no hope. That is the way the book sounds. Nothing can be done. There is no use praying. It is too late to pray. God will not listen to prayer—not for Judah. The Ethiopian cannot change his skin. The leopard cannot change his spots. There is no balm in Gilead. There is no physician there. That is the way the book reads—if you read it on the surface. Dante saw inscribed over the entrance into hell the awful words, "All hope abandon ye who enter here." That is the inscription which many read written across the Book of Jeremiah.

Let me now show you what an encouraging book it is. Let me point out the gleams of hope which come flashing through its somber paragraphs. Let us read the book with our eyes open. Let us endeavor to get beneath the surface. The book says that to-day is dark. It says to-morrow will be dark. It says that some day after that it will be light. It says there is always light ahead. Did you ever notice the expression, "I will not make a full end of you." It occurs five times in the book, in chapters four and five and thirty and forty-six. It is always put into the mouth of God. It is something which God says. Jeremiah is sure of that. In the fourth chapter there is an appalling picture of destruction. The earth will mourn. The heavens will be black. The whole population will flee from the city. Some of them will plunge into the thickets and others will climb the sides of mountains and try to hide in the caves in the rocks. Every city will be forsaken and the whole land will be desolate. But right in the midst of this dark prediction, God lifts up his voice and says, "I will not make a full end." The destruction will be complete, but it shall not be final. The ruin will be awful, but it shall not be irremediable. In the fifth chapter the picture of catastrophe is again vivid. The invading army will eat up the harvest fields, and the flocks and the herds and the vines and the fig trees. The walls of the fortified cities will be beaten down. Then comes a flash of hope. "But even in those days," saith Jehovah, "I will not make a full end with you." The destruction will be terrible, but it will not be annihilating. The desolation will be

[199]

heartbreaking, but it will be transitory. This suffering is a semicolon in the unfolding story of God's people; it is not the end of a sentence, it is not a period. It is dark to-day, and it will be dark to-morrow, but there is light farther on.

In the thirtieth chapter the same idea is sounded this time through the throats of trumpets. "Do not fear, O Jacob! Do not be dismayed, O Israel! I am with you. I will save you. I will make a full end of all the nations whither I have scattered you, but I will not make a full end of you!" The chastisement will be severe, but it will not be without limit. At the end of chapter forty-six, the same motif is introduced again. At first it had been played by only a few instruments, but now it is taken up by the full orchestra, and the glorious truth is repeated once again as if the prophet wished the music of that jubilant hope to linger in the ear—"I will not make a full end with you!"

There is another expression which should not be overlooked—"seventy years." It is an expression put into the mouth of God. It is something which God says. He says that the authority of the King of Babylon is a limited authority. Conscienceless despotism cannot lord it over the nations forever. Tyranny can continue for a season, but soon it shall be cut off. "After seventy years I will punish the King of Babylon, and I will overthrow his kingdom with an everlasting devastation. No matter what despot sits upon the throne there is always light ahead.

In the twenty-ninth chapter this hope comes shining through again. God is now talking of the people. He assures them that after seventy years he will visit them, and will cause them to return to their native land.

This is a promise which comes creeping in again and again. It takes many forms and expresses itself in a variety of figures. In the third chapter it takes this form: "I will take one man out of a city and two men out of a clan and bring them to Zion!" In the twenty-third chapter, it takes a different form: "I will gather the remnant of my flock out of all the countries whither I have driven them. I will bring them again to their folds. I will set up shepherds over them who shall feed them. They shall not be afraid. Not one of them will be missing." The captivity is galling, but it is limited. It is dark to-day, but there is light ahead.

In the twenty-seventh chapter the prophet is speaking to Zedekiah. He reminds him of what took place in the reign of his predecessor. He refers to the golden vessels which the king of Babylon had taken from the temple and carried

to his capitol. The prophet goes on to say that
the King of Babylon is coming again. The next
time he will carry off all the sacred vessels. He
will take them to Babylon where they will remain
for many years, but they will not remain there
forever. "I will bring them back," says Jehovah.
"I will restore them to the place from which they
were taken."

In the thirty-second chapter the prediction becomes still bolder. Not only will the sacred vessels be brought back, but the people themselves
will return. God is going to gather them out of
all the countries whither he has driven them, and
he will cause them to dwell in their former home
securely. "They shall be my people and I will
be their God. I will plant them in this land with
my whole heart and with my whole soul." The
captivity will be long and dreadful, but it will
come to an end. It is dark in this generation. It
will be dark in the next, but farther on it will be
light. There is always light ahead.

This is wonderful. Let us pause and look at
it. Let us meditate on it. Let us gaze on this
man afire with hope. Many persons have difficulty
in believing in the inspiration of the Bible. The
idea of inspiration is to them repellent. They
find it especially hard to believe in the inspiration
of the Old Testament. Why should the Hebrew

prophets have been inspired? Now and then some one ventures the assertion that they were no more inspired than Shakespeare. It is interesting to note how often Shakespeare is lugged in. It seems easier to admit the inspiration of the Hebrew prophets if you concede that Shakespeare was inspired. Some people assert that the prophets were no more inspired than we are. That makes it easy to believe in Biblical inspiration. If everybody is inspired, it is not hard to believe the prophets were inspired. If you bring us all into one class, then the doctrine of inspiration becomes credible!

But what is inspiration? It is difficult to frame a definition which some one will not cavil at. Let us look at the thing itself. Here is an instance of it. Here is an authentic exhibition of it. Let us look it squarely in the face. It is a dark hour in the history of the world. The human race has reached a crisis in its career. It was midnight and at that midnight hour, this man Jeremiah was doomed to look upon the three greatest tragedies which the human imagination can conceive. He saw the Temple of God burned to the ground. It was an old temple, hundreds of years old, and all the more precious because of its age. It was a magnificent temple, built by King Solomon, the most beautiful and costly temple in all the East.

It was a revered temple, dear to every pious Hebrew heart, worshiped almost to the verge of idolatry, the most hallowed thing in all the world. He saw this architectural wonder, this shrine of the Eternal reduced to a heap of ashes. He saw it fall, and he said, "There will be another temple."

He saw the City of Jerusalem demolished. It was the capital of his country. It was the only large and opulent city in all Judah. It was the City of King David, the City of the great King. The bold Isaiah had said only a hundred years before that Jerusalem could not be captured, that it was inviolable, under the special protection of the King of Heaven, and yet this city fell. Jeremiah saw it fall. He saw it demolished so that there was not a stone left standing on another. He gazed on the rubbish heap of what had once been called "Jerusalem," and said "There will be another city."

He saw his country broken into fragments and all the fragments scattered. He saw his countrymen, some of them butchered and the others dragged off into captivity. He saw them going. He said "They will come back again." Before Jeremiah's day ten tribes had gone into captivity and no one of them had come back again. Now the remaining two tribes are going, and he, nothing daunted, said, "They will come back again! There will be a new temple, a new city, a new nation. There is light ahead!"

This is wonderful. You ought to think about it a long time. It is one of the most amazing spectacles in the history of the world. Here is a man out under a midnight sky. There is no moon and all the stars are dead. He stares into the darkness and keeps on staring until he sees on the far distant horizon a tiny tinge of light. Here is a man who in the darkest night which ever fell upon a land, carried the dawn in his eyes.

It was winter. A chilling blast was blowing across the world. All the flowers were dead, and all the buds were shriveled. There was not a blade of green grass visible anywhere. Here is a man who walks across a field of ice with the summer in his heart.

It was a night of tempest. A fearful storm was raging, the most terrific storm which ever tore its way across the affrighted world. It blew out the lights one after another until they all were out— all but one, the light which burned in just one man's soul. The light of hope. It flickered in the hurricane, it died down, it seemed at times almost to be extinguished, but it burned on, it never went out. Hope had kindled a fire which could not be extinguished.

The world was falling to pieces, civilization was collapsing, the social order was disintegrating, everything was sinking down into chaos and night, but here is a man who in the midst of the thunder and uproar continues to sing. That is inspiration! Where did this hope come from? Not from the beasts, for the animals have no hope. Not from his countrymen, for his countrymen were hopeless. Where did it come from? Why not say it came from God? Is not that the most reasonable answer? What is inspiration? It is the inbreathing into the human spirit of the spirit of God. It is the infiltration into the human mind of the Divine mind. It is the shining through into the human soul of the glory of the Eternal.

Jeremiah was a man of hope because he was very sure of God. He clung fast to God. When you overhear Jeremiah talking to God in hours which are especially dark, you hear him saying, "O thou hope of Israel!" You never heard that expression before. You never caught it from the lips of any prophet or priest or king. This is a new name for God, a name coined in the mint of Jeremiah's mind. There is no hope aside from God. God is the God of hope, the fountain of hope, and the sustainer of it. Twenty-four hun-

dred years after Jeremiah's day, Charles Wesley
wrote:

> "Other refuge have I none;
> Hangs my helpless soul on Thee;
> Leave, ah! leave me not alone,
> Still support and comfort me.
> All my trust on Thee is stayed,
> All my help from Thee I bring;
> Cover my defenseless head
> With the shadow of Thy wing!"

That prayer was uttered in the sixth century before Christ by Jeremiah when he prayed, "O
Lord, the hope of Israel, heal me and I shall be
healed; save me and I shall be saved!"

Every man has his favorite name for God.
The favorite name of God with Paul was, "The
God and Father of our Lord Jesus Christ," but
there were times when he cast it aside to take up
another. In his letter to the Romans he falls back
on the conception of Jeremiah. Paul was keenly
sensitive to the magic of language and was highly
appreciative of the lofty flights of the human
mind, and he loved the name which Jeremiah had
given to God six hundred years before. You can
hear the voice of Jeremiah in Paul's benediction,
"Now may the God of Hope fill you with all joy
and peace in believing that ye may abound in
hope."

Paul was a great admirer of Jeremiah. He had Jeremiah's book by heart. The blood of Jeremiah's ideas ran through the veins of Paul's brain. Jesus also loved him. He fed his mind on the truths which the prophet had spoken, he braced his spirit by commuming with the prophet's soul. You cannot read the letters of Paul without feeling sure that Paul and Jeremiah were companions, and you cannot read the Gospels without feeling confident that Jesus had lingered long over the pages of Jeremiah. In many respects Jesus and Jeremiah were much alike. They were alike in their outward fortunes. They were both fated to have their hearts wrung by unspeakable tragedies. Jeremiah saw with his eyes the burning of the temple, the destruction of Jerusalem, and the scattering of the Hebrew nation. Jesus in his mind's eye saw the same overwhelming calamities. To his vision the coming years were unveiled. He saw the burning of the temple and the downfall of the city, and the dispersion of the people. But like Jeremiah he was not daunted. He did not fall into despair. The flame of hope was never in him extinguished. He knew it was dark to-day, and that it would be dark to-morrow, but he was sure there was light ahead. One day he said to his disciples: "I am going to Jerusalem and there I shall suffer many things. I shall be rejected by the elders and the priests. I shall be killed. But on the third day I shall rise." The disciples were so stunned by the predictions concerning suffering and death that they did not hear what he said about the resurrection. They were thrown into despair because they stopped at a semicolon. They failed to listen to Jesus until he had reached the period. They saw the darkness to-day and shuddered at the coming darkness of to-morrow, but they failed to see the light which was shining farther on. Jesus saw the light ahead. "For the joy that was set before him he endured the cross."

On his way to Jerusalem he was attended by a company of doleful and downhearted disciples. The sky was black and growing blacker all the time. All round the horizon there hung thunder-clouds and the lightnings flashed again and again. The hearts of the disciples were terror-stricken, but he calmly said, "Fear not little flock, it is your Father's good pleasure to give you the Kingdom." His hope was still bright.

When he arrived in Jerusalem the city was a seething caldron of hate. He was the great lover. He lived only to teach men how to love. He longed to have them love him. But they hated him. Nothing that he said or did had induced them to give him their hearts. They hated him more and more. Jerusalem was a nest of serpents. The serpents hissed at him every hour of the day, but right in the midst of the hissing he said, "I, if I be lifted up, will draw all men unto me." "I have not drawn anybody yet except this handful of disciples, but when I die I shall begin to draw men to me, and I shall keep on drawing them until the whole world is mine." He was saved by hope.

In the upper chamber on the last night he looked into the sad eyes of his despondent friends and said, "Be of good cheer, I have overcome the world." He had not overcome any part of it yet. He had not conquered Jerusalem or Judea or Samaria or Galilee or Greece or Rome, but nevertheless he kept on hoping. He was confident of ultimate victory. "Be of good cheer. I have overcome the world."

After he had passed the bread and the wine, and had requested them to think of him every time they ate and drank, he said just before they sang a closing Psalm, "I shall not drink henceforth of this fruit of the vine until that day when I drink it new with you in my Father's Kingdom." It was a dark night, and it would be darker in the morning, but he would not allow them to forget that there was light ahead. "In my Father's house are many mansions, I go to prepare a place for you."

That is what he said and says. The valley of the shadow of death is dark, but there is light ahead!

What is the weakest spot, do you think, in our Christian character? Where are we most defective? Sometimes one thinks we are weakest in our faith. We have little faith. We have sometimes no faith at all. We stand with the man at the foot of the Mount of Transfiguration and say, "Lord we believe, help thou our unbelief."

But sometimes it seems we are most lacking in our love. We do not love enough. We do not know how to love. Our love is thin and feeble. It lacks fire and therefore is devoid of joy and power. We are loveless Christians and that is why we are impotent when it comes to casting out demons.

But there are times when I am convinced that our crowning defect is our hopelessness. We do not know how to hope. We do not even know what hope is. We have emptied all the great words of the New Testament of their contents. We have degraded the holiest words. We have made faith mean the acceptance of a proposition, and we have made love an empty sentiment, and we have made hope equivalent to a wish. We use the word hope only in cheap and insignificant situations. We hope it will not rain, and we hope our investments will come out all right, and we hope our favorite candidate will be elected. But we do not hope for the great things, the glorious things which Christians in this world ought to hope for. We do not hope that our city will become the City of God. We do not expect that. The city is too big and too wicked. How could a big and wicked city like New York become the City of God? But that is one of the things we are to hope for. It is dark to-day, and it will be dark to-morrow, but there is always light ahead. The present city may be destroyed and its successor may be blotted out, but sometime and somehow there is going to be on Manhattan Island a City of God.

We do not hope for our country. We do not expect the American people to become the people of God. They are too materialistic, too sordid, too selfish, too worldly-minded. They can never become the people of God. Yet that is one of the things we are to hope for. It is indeed dark to-day and will be dark to-morrow, but there is always light ahead.

We have no hope for Europe, poor, wrangling, hate-cursed war-bedeviled Europe. Who could have any hope of Europe coming into the Kingdom of God? And we have still less hope for Africa, and less still for Asia. All the continents are hopeless.

We do not hope that there will ever be heaven on earth. And yet that is the very thing which Jeremiah hoped for. We hope for heaven on the other side of death. We are slackers and choose the easiest course. It is easier to dream heaven on the other side of death than to create heaven on this side of it. To create heaven on this planet is our job. That is why we are here. Jeremiah knew nothing of the other world, apparently cared nothing for it, never mentioned it in any of his recorded sermons. He believed that heaven can exist here, and that it is going to exist here. It is dark to-day and will be dark to-morrow, but there is always light ahead.

Jesus adopted the idea of Jeremiah. Jesus believed that heaven could exist here. He declared with passionate enthusiasm that heaven is at hand. He told men always to put at the forefront of their petitions, "Thy Kingdom come, thy will be done on earth as it is done in heaven." That is the chief thing we are to pray for—heaven on earth. "And in your work," he went on to say, "always aim at bringing heaven to earth. Seek ye first the Kingdom of God, and you have solved all the problems. Seek heaven. Every one who seeks finds." Such is the good news. We are to work for heaven on earth.

Cling close to Jesus of Nazareth the greatest

lover and also the greatest hoper who has ever lived. And keep close also to Jeremiah who stands next to the Son of God in his capacity for hoping. Never think of Jeremiah as sitting amid the ruins of the temple, with the tears running down his cheeks, pleading with a sobbing voice for all the generations to pity him and his unhappy people. Think of him always as standing in the midst of the ruins of the capital of his country with the Temple of King Solomon a mass of débris at his feet, a heavenly fire in his eyes, and saying in a tone which thrills, "There is going to be a new temple, and a new city, and a new nation, and a new world, because God is going to give man a new heart!"

APPENDIX

ONE HUNDRED QUESTIONS ON THE BOOK OF JEREMIAH

For the Use of Bible Classes

1. Compare the Book of Jeremiah with those of Isaiah and Ezekiel in size, literary quality and religious value.
2. How does the Septuagint translation of this book differ from the Hebrew?
3. On what principle are its contents arranged?
4. In what respects is the book unique?
5. What is its chief treasure?
6. What section of the book is called the "Book of Consolation"?
7. What other books in the Old Testament have been ascribed to Jeremiah?
8. What reasons are there for thinking he did not write the "Lamentations"?
9. What Old Testament book bears the deepest marks of the influence of Jeremiah?
10. Is the Book of Jeremiah interesting to you? Is it hard to read?
11. When and where was Jeremiah born? When and where did he die?
12. What did he attempt to do, and what did he accomplish?

55. Who was the successor of Jeremiah?
56. Was Jeremiah a theologian? Did he have a creed?
57. What three ideas run through all the Hebrew prophets?
58. What was Jeremiah's conception of God? Wherein did it fall short of the conception of Jesus?
59. What was his idea of the Messiah, and how did it differ from that of Isaiah?
60. How did his picture of the future differ from those of Isaiah and Micah?
61. State his doctrine of predestination.
62. What did he learn in a pottery?
63. Compare Paul's use of the potter with that of Jeremiah.
64. Has he anything to teach us concerning the Holy Spirit? Immortality?
65. Did he expect heaven on earth? Do you?
66. What is his most original and crowning idea?
67. Make a list of his fulfilled predictions. A list also of his predictions unfulfilled.
68. What was his conception of man?
69. What was his doctrine of sin?
70. What was his idea of patriotism?
71. If Jesus is all-sufficient, why do we need Jeremiah?
72. What is the difference between a Reformation and a Revival?
73. Can civil law further the interests of religion? Of morality?
74. What was the supreme problem of Jeremiah? Of Paul? Of Job?
75. How did the New Testament get its name?

76. How does an Old Testament saint differ from a New Testament saint?

77. How did the Hebrew conception of God differ from that of the other Semitic tribes?

78. How did the Hebrew literary conventions differ from ours?

79. What is a prophetic ministry? Do we want one?

80. Why speak for God if in speaking we bring scorn on ourselves and hardness of heart in our hearers?

81. Is it our duty to avoid controversy? Strife? Pain? Unpopularity?

82. How may the Bible become a curse?

83. What important changes have the Revisers made?

84. How can the repetitions in the book be accounted for?

85. What is the one thing indispensable in Religion?

86. Why does Jeremiah come closer to us than any other Hebrew prophet?

87. How can we strengthen ourselves to bear loneliness? Misunderstanding? Persecution?

88. Is Zionism a hopeless enterprise?

89. Will the Jews ever come to Christ?

90. How was Palestine lost? Can the United States be lost?

91. What do you think of our national Christianity?

92. What were the social abuses of Judah? What are ours?

93. What is a national sin?

94. What are our national sins?

95. What is a church sin? What are ours?

96. Should we mix politics and religion? Religion and business?

97. Should preachers go into politics? Should laymen? Should the church?
98. Should the pulpit take an interest in foreign policy?
99. What is the chief value of this book in our generation?
100. How has the study of the book helped you to become a better citizen? A better Christian?